AMERICA
THEN & NOW

AMERICA
THEN & NOW

SHERRY MARKER

BARNES
&NOBLE
BOOKS
NEW YORK

This edition published by
Barnes & Noble, Inc.,
by arrangement with Brompton Books
Corporation.

Produced by Brompton Books Corporation
15 Sherwood Place
Greenwich, CT 06830

ISBN 1-56619-221-8

Printed in Italy

Front jacket: The Manhattan skyline
viewed from under the Brooklyn Bridge,
now (left) and 50 years ago (right).

Back jacket: *By columns, left to right:* The
Chicago River, 1930 and today; West
Point cadets, 1888 and today; Yosemite
Park, 1904 and today; a Boston swan
boat, 1926 and today.

Page 1: *Below:* A modern hi-tech fire
engine. *Above:* A 1910 fire truck pulling a
pump-and-horse wagon.

Previous pages: *Left:* Manhattan and the
Brooklyn Bridge in 1908. *Right:*
Manhattan and the Brooklyn Bridge
today.

This page: *Above:* The 1992 Democratic
presidential convention in New York City
nominates Bill Clinton. *Below:* The 1900
Democratic presidential convention in
Kansas City nominates William Jennings
Bryan.

CONTENTS

INTRODUCTION

It is almost impossible to overstate the importance of photography in our daily lives. We are bombarded incessantly by photographic images – on TV, in movie theaters, in our newspapers, magazines, and books – that shape our sense of ourselves, our country, and the world. And, to a degree we sometimes fail to realize, these images also shape our sense of the past.

Before the advent of the photograph historical iconography was exclusively the domain of the artist, a fact has left us heir both to quite a lot of impressive art and to a great many unresolved – and probably unresolvable – questions of fact. Consider a case in point. There are two faces that almost every American school-child can identify: George Washington and Abraham Lincoln. Each man has been portrayed in various ways, but the standard images are those used on our currency. Washington gazes serenely at us from every $1 bill, and Lincoln, more introspectively, from every $5 bill. We owe the image of Washington mainly to the painter Gilbert Stuart, who virtually supported himself by turning out copies of his own portraits of Washington. Our image of Lincoln is based almost entirely on photographs, mostly those of Matthew Brady, whose camera also brought images of the Civil War into homes across the nation.

From the historical point of view, the difference is considerable. We really don't know whether Stuart's idealized portrait is a good likeness of the first president, and a considerable body of modern scholarship has suggested that it may not be. But even if we knew for certain that Stuart had misrepresented his subject, we should still lack any demonstrably more authentic image. By the time of Lincoln, however, not a hundred years later, photography was available and everything was changed. Today we do not have to rely on words or paint for our image of the sixteenth president; we have a small gallery of photographic images of the man himself.

Before photography many of the visual images of America were recorded by artists like those itinerant painters, many anonymous, who traveled about portraying the families, farms, homes, and landscapes of the new nation. These self-taught artisans were most numerous in the more settled parts of the country, and most of their surviving work was done in the Northeast, especially in the hamlets and towns of the Hudson and Connecticut River Valleys. Such paintings provide fascinating social history, offering glimpses of the material culture – the clothes, books, furniture, tools – of early America. But if they are accurate in general, they are almost never wholly accurate in their particulars. The people who commissioned the paintings wanted to be flattered – wanted their houses to look bigger and cleaner than they were, wanted their fields to look broader and richer, their herds fatter, themselves handsomer and better dressed – and the artists obliged. And not only the itinerant artists: most artists. A little-known nineteenth-century poet, Fitz-Green Halleck, wrote Thomas Hicks, the Philadelphia portraitist who was about to paint him: "I want you to paint me so that I shall look like a gentleman. Never mind the likeness. In fifty

Opposite and above: The corners of Randolph and Dearborn Sts. in Chicago, in 1905 and as it looks today. Then a busy intersection, it was jammed with traffic. Now it is the site of a featureless new parking lot.

Left: A mid-1930s view of San Francisco. The San Francisco-Oakland Bridge (foreground) and the Golden Gate Bridge are both still being built.

Opposite: San Francisco now, looking over the Golden Gate Bridge toward the city and the bridge to Oakland.

8

years nobody will be able to tell whether the portrait is a likeness or not, but I want to be handed down to posterity as a gentleman." In all likelihood the only thing that might have surprised Hicks about this request was its candor; flattering sitters was tacitly understood to be part of his job, his bread and butter.

The unflattering eye of the camera has been available to record history for only a relatively brief period, but in that time its contribution has been decisive. In 1993 that contribution to our understanding of the past was recognized by New York's Metropolitan Museum of Art, which mounted an exhibit on photography's first century. As the Metropolitan Museum's photography curator, Maria Morris Hambourg, put it, photography has given us "privileged seats in the memory theater of the world."

The first photographs were taken in 1826 by the Frenchman Joseph Nicephore Niepce, who successfully exposed and recorded an image on a light-sensitive plate inside a camera obscura, essentially just a box with a lens. In 1839 another Frenchman, Louis J. M. Daguerre, a former partner of Niepce, made a major step forward in photographic technique: Daguerre exposed a light-sensitive plate and then developed and "fixed" the image with chemical compounds. The result was known as the "daguerreotype." At about the same time, British scientist William H. F. Talbot devised a light-sensitive paper that,

when treated with chemicals, served as a negative from which a positive print could be made and then fixed with other chemicals. Almost all early photographs taken by these processes tended to be of inanimate structures because of the requirement that a subject had to hold still for many minutes in order for the image to be "caught." When people posed for portraits, neck-braces helped them to hold still—and often made them look exceptionally somber, since it was nearly impossible to hold a smile long enough to be photographed.

Within months, American newspapers carried reports of Daguerre and Talbot's photographic inventions, and by the end of the 1840s almost every American town had its Daguerrian studio, where entire families posed for each other and for posterity. Photographers also took their clumsy cameras out and about, leaving us images of New England sailing ships, the Boston Common, and unpaved streets in towns from New York to San Francisco. In 1851 Englishman Frederick Scott Archer devised the "wet plate" process, which soon made the daguerreotype obsolete. This was the process Matthew Brady used for his Civil War photographs and for his photos of Abraham Lincoln. But perhaps the greatest break-through in photography came when American George Eastman devised first the dry-plate process and then the Kodak camera (1888), which held a compact roll of film capable of recording multiple images. Such rapid

technical progress made it possible for American photography to compile an impressive archive of images in the second half of the nineteenth century, an archive that would soon be dwarfed by that accumulated in the century that followed.

This book has drawn on hundreds of photos, taken by both professional and amateur photographers, to create something of an unofficial national family album that we can look through to see how we have changed – and how we have not – during the last 100 or so years. In these pages are recorded images of a time when people on horseback could casually ride about the streets of New York City. Here the reader will find scenes both of the first trolleycars in Los Angeles and of the city's automobile-snarled freeways today. Old and new photographs

similarly document the dramatic changes that have taken place in other aspects of our lives – in our workplaces, in our big cities and small towns, in our costumes and our tastes in art and architecture.

By the same token, many of the "then" and "now" photographs in this book convey a message that is mainly one of continuity, reminding us that in some ways we have changed remarkably little. The clothes passengers wear in the swan boats on the pond in the Boston Botanical Garden may have changed, but the boats and the gardens look essentially as they did in the 1880s. And in towns such as Taos, New Mexico, or Hot Springs and Eureka Springs, Arkansas, there are streets where residents from the turn of the century would feel much at home. To be sure, some places that seem unchanged have, in fact, been artfully

preserved, usually as tourist attractions. Almost all of Deadwood, South Dakota, has been maintained this way, and even in areas of explosive urban growth old factories and markets, such as Boston's Quincy Market, much of Baltimore's old port, and New York City's South Sea Seaport, have been saved from destruction and converted to new uses.

The preservation movement in America has grown enormously in recent years, fueled by a realization that the urban renewal projects of the 1950s and 1960s often leveled historic buildings and homes that were an important part of the national heritage. Preservationists saw to it that much of Charleston, South Carolina's, ante-bellum glory was preserved from developers, and when nature, in the shape of Hurricane Hugo, devastated much of Charleston in 1989, preservationists again rallied to recreate much familiar local monuments as the steeple of Saint Michael's church. To be sure, some people have said that the preservationist pendulum may have swung too far when, for example, Floridians band together to save an "architecturally undistinguished" school from the 1930s, or when the garish Grauman's Chinese Theater in Los Angeles is declared a protected building. But such critics would do well to remember that probably the worst criterion of any building's historic value is whether it conforms to contemporary taste – as many New Yorkers who now mourn the loss of the old Pennsylvania Station would willingly attest.

Our nation has grown at such a rate that the early photographers could record many scenes of undeveloped and uninhabited countryside that is now overdeveloped and overpopulated. The sites of Las Vegas, Reno, and Miami Beach, for example, were until fairly recently considered to be wastelands, unprofitable and virtually uninhabitable. Now, in their different ways, they are symbols of glamor (or, at any rate, glitz) and of the American ability to create towns that can give the illusion of broad daylight 24 hours a day. That same American readiness to transform the face of nature has also produced such engineering triumphs as the Hoover and Grand Coulee Dams and such elegantly soaring structures as the Brooklyn and Golden Gate Bridges. All these, too, have been captured in "then-and-now" images that have an important place in our national family album.

11

Probably the most celebrated bridge in the nation is New York's Brooklyn Bridge: Walt Whitman and Hart Crane were but two of its many literary partisans. The photo right – taken about 1870 – shows the bridge in an early stage of its construction. The photo opposite confirms that this elegant span has lost none of its fabled magic today.

THE NORTHEAST

No single image conjurs up the Northeast in the same way that magnolias and plantations suggest the South, or fields of corn and wheat symbolize the Midwest. That is because the Northeast is in some ways a microcosm of the entire United States, with mountains and seashore, wilderness trails and superhighways, church steeples and skyscrapers, communities of Native Americans and neighborhoods where Spanish or Korean are heard as often as English. The Northeast includes all of New England, along with New York, New Jersey, and Pennsylvania – even though some New Yorkers admit to no regional identification beyond their own state, some New Jerseyites think of themselves as having a good deal in common with their mid-Atlantic neighbors in Delaware and Maryland, and many western Pennsylvanians regard "the East" with more than a little suspicion.

Yet even though "the Northeast" might be regarded by some as an arbitrary construct, the area does have both a shared history and certain highly specific regional characteristics, starting with the land itself. Hills and mountains, essentially all part of the Appalachian chain, run across the Northeast from Maine to Pennsylvania, and a coast cut by deep harbors stretches along the Atlantic from New Jersey to Maine. Numerous rivers – the Connecticut, Housatonic, Hudson, Delaware, Susquehanna, and Allegheny – crisscross the Northeast from the mountains and lakes of the north, some flowing into the Atlantic, others winding west into the neighboring Midwest, and others south to the Gulf of Mexico.

It is not surprising that the Northeast is the region that comes most to mind when people think of the beginnings of the United States. After all, the second permanent English settlement (after Jamestown, Virginia) was at Plymouth, Massachusetts. The Nation's first major cities were Boston, Philadelphia, and New York. And most of the formative events from the colonial period through the Revolution took place in the Northeast.

In the nineteenth century much of the rural landscape of the Northeast was transformed by the Industrial Revolution. As early as 1793, Samuel Slater's Pawtucket, Rhode Island, textile mill had imported the techniques of the Industrial Revolution from England to the United States, and soon the whole American textile industry had converted to mass production on water-powered looms. In the 1820s Lowell, Massachusetts, was built as the nation's first factory city designed to avoid the inhuman working conditions of England's "dark, Satanic mills." In New Jersey, Patterson grew from the small town into an industrial center turning out Colt revolvers, cotton, and so much silk that it was nicknamed "The Silk City."

Beginning in 1837, locomotives were also manufactured in Patterson, for now the railroad was beginning to replace canals, rivers, and roads as the most efficient means of transportation. Soon, all across the Northeast cities such as Newark, New Jersey, Hartford, Connecticut, Springfield, Massachusetts,

Opposite: In 1968 the anonymous facade of Madison Square Garden Center rose on the site previously occupied by Pennsylvania Station's baroque splendor. Trains are now relegated to the complex's lowest level, with offices and the Madison Square Garden sports and entertainment center taking up the rest of the nine storeys. Madison Square Garden is home to the New York's basketball team, the Knickerbockers, and its ice hockey team, the Rangers. In addition, every year Madison Square Garden hosts special events, from the International Antiques Show and the Ringling Brothers, Barnum & Bailey Circus to rock concerts and the Westminster Dog Show.

Above: Many of New York City's most elegant turn-of-the-century buildings, such as the Municipal Building, the Morgan Library, and the Fifth Avenue wings of the Metropolitan Museum of Art, were designed by the distinguished firm of McKim, Mead & White. One of their most distinguished and beloved buildings was Pennsylvania Station, which dominated the Garment District from 1910 until it was torn down in 1968. Modeled on the baths of Caracalla, Penn Station was a frank statement of New York's energy and self-confidence. Lamenting the change from Penn Station's grandeur to the merely functional train station buried deep within the Madison Square Garden complex, architecture historian Vincent Scully said that while the traveler once entered the city "like a god . . . One scuttles in now like a rat."

14

Saratoga Springs was one of the country's most fashionable spas at the turn of the century (above). When visitors tired of taking the waters, they could gamble at the Casino or bet at the Saratoga Race Track, scene of the Travers Cup, America's oldest horse race.

The hansom cabs and the private railroad cars that notables such as Diamond Jim Brady used here are long since gone, but Saratoga Springs today (right) retains much of its charm. Some 900 of its buildings are listed on the National Register of Historic Places.

Albany, New York, and Harrisburg, Pennsylvania, would be linked by rail.

When oil was discovered in Pennsylvania in 1857 the "Keystone State" was well on its way to becoming one of the great industrial centers in the country. By the 1870s Pittsburgh would produce not only most of the nation's, but much of the world's, steel, while boasting that it was the Northeast's "Gateway to the West." Indeed, at this time all three of the country's most important manufacturing centers – Pittsburgh, Lowell, and Fall River (Massachusetts) – were in the Northeast.

But more than any of these, one city in the Northeast came to symbolize urban America: New York. In population, variety, and commercial importance – even in sheer height – New York had no rivals. In 1857 the first elevator was installed in a Manhattan building, and by the 1870s that paradigm of modern urban architecture, the skyscraper, was well on its way to transforming New York's already lofty skyline into one of the wonders of the world.

The fulminating growth of the Northeast did not really abate until the 1930s. The Great Depression had tragic consequences for many in the region, with factories shutting down and small businesses failing everywhere. Perhaps only the intervention of the New Deal government saved the area from ruin.

It was not until the decades following World War II that the Northeast was revitalized and began to assume its contemporary aspect. Cheap automobiles and good roads allowed the middle class to escape urban constraints and to relocate in suburban housing developments such as Long Island's Levittown. "Ring roads" such as Boston's Route 128 became crowded with factories and offices that chose to locate outside the center cities. Shopping malls sprang up to serve the suburbanites, who increasingly went into the cities only to work, or to enjoy the cultural riches of the theaters, symphonies, and museums that had been founded in the cities' heyday.

The middle class was not alone in leaving the cities: many industries either relocated in the South, where labor was cheaper, or moved overseas. The urban poor, often ill-trained for the new "high tech" jobs that were increasingly in demand in industry, were often trapped in a cycle of unemployment – or underemployment – that was passed from generation to generation.

The last hundred years, then, has brought profound – and often disquieting – change to the Northeast. But there is also much that remains unchanged. There are still small towns, from colonial Old Wethersfield, Connecticut, to Victorian Cape May, New Jersey, that remain almost as they were when they were first settled. And the dairy-farm country along Route 20 in upstate New York, the gentle farmland of Lancaster County, Pennsylvania, and a wide swath of ruggedly picturesque farmland in New England still very successfully hold the invasive superhighways and shopping malls at bay. And every year visitors from all over the world come to view the most changeless thing of all in the Northeast: the dazzling glory of New England's autumn foliage.

15

Only about 1000 people live year-round in Kennebunkport, Maine. Often that many visitors arrive on a single summer day to visit this seaside resort that still suggests something of the working fishing village it until recently was (above). There now may be more yachts than lobster boats in the harbor (right), and shops in Dock Square sell souvenirs rather than fishing tackle, but it is easy to see why vacationers such as former President George Bush come here each year. Like many New England towns, Kennebunkport prides itself less on change than on changelessness.

Above and left: Like Kennebunkport, Vinalhaven Island, one of Maine's Penobscot Bay islands, has some 1000 year-round residents. Unlike Kennebunkport, the island has yet to become chic, though many day-trippers visit the island in the summer. Lobstering is still the main source of income here, and lobster traps and lobster boats still dominate the harbor docks. Well into this century Vinalhaven's granite quarries supplied stone for some of the country's best-known buildings, including the Cathedral of Saint John the Divine in New York City; now many of the abandoned quarries are popular local swimming holes.

Right: Gloucester harbor, as it looked a half-century ago. Located on the Cape Ann peninsula north of Boston, the town may be America's oldest fishing port, for it was established in 1623. By the nineteenth century the Gloucester fleet was scouring the Atlantic for cod and mackrel, which were shipped all over the world; indeed, this famous fleet was the inspiration for Kipling's novel *Captains Courageous*. Fishing is still the main industry here (right, below), but the town has also always attracted artists. One such was Fitz Hugh Lane, many of whose seascapes are on view at the Cape Ann Historical Society. A few miles from Gloucester, on the tip of Cape Ann, Rockport is less of a fishing village than an artists' colony where art galleries and boutiques line the seaside streets. One weathered red fishing shed (opposite), that never became a boutique or restaurant, was painted by artists so often it was nicknamed "Motif No. 1."

20

While the fishing fleets of Gloucester were searching for cod, mackrel, and halibut, the ships of Nantucket Island, Massachusetts, hunted whales. In the eighteenth and nineteenth centuries Nantucket was the center of the world's whaling industry, shipping barrels of oil everywhere in America and across the Atlantic, and whaling money built the handsome mansions and shops that still line Nantucket's Main Street. But after petroleum began to replace whale oil in the 1860s, the whaling industry declined, and with it Nantucket's prosperity. The island's isolation protected it from development, however, and its old-fashioned charm had, by the late nineteenth century, made it into a favored vacation spot. Today, bicycles and cars have replaced the horse-drawn waggons that rolled down Main Street in the 1890s (opposite), but, especially on the narrow cobbled side streets, some still with gas street lights (above), Nantucket today looks very much as it did 100 years ago. Guest houses and small hotels in town, and condominiums and resorts discreetly tucked away outside, proclaim the island's current source of income. As for the whales that brought Nantucket its original prosperity, they are remembered in the island's Whaling Museum, housed in a former factory where candles were once made from whale oil.

Right: As Boston expanded it first grew out, and then it grew up. By the late 1700s the city, sometimes called "the Cradle of Independence" and "the Athens of America," had outgrown its original site on the Shawmut peninsula. In the next 100 years much of Back and South Bays were filled in to create more land as the city spread south.

In the 1860s (photo right) and well into this century, the Boston skyline was low and harmonious, broken only by church steeples. Some of the finest, such as Trinity Church on Copley Square, were designed by the architect Henry Hobson Richardson in the Romanesque style which he helped to popularize.

Left: A few blocks from historic Trinity Church, are some of today's best-known symbols of the "new Boston:" the Prudential Center with its Prudential Tower, the city's second-tallest skyscraper. The Prudential Center complex constitutes a small town: 32 acres of shops, apartments, offices, banks, food stores, and restaurants — even an ice skating rink. Although the Prudential Center profoundly changed the face of Boston, it also pulled the city together, linking the Back Bay and South End neighborhoods, which had previously been divided by sprawling railroad yards.

24

Fifty years before landscape architect Frederick Law Olmsted designed Boston's splendid network of parks, the city's "emerald necklace," one centerpiece of that necklace was already in place. Created in 1837 adjacent to the Common, Boston's Public Garden was America's first public botanical garden. Ever since, it has been a haven of tranquility in the heart of a busy, ever-changing metropolis. How little the Garden has changed in this century is suggested by the two photos of the central pond and its famous swan boats on the right — one a contemporary shot and the other taken in the 1920s.

Unlike others parts of Boston, where marshes were filled *in* to create new land, in the Public Garden the marsh was dug *out* to create a pond. On it, since 1877, the colorful, pedal-powered swan boats have plied their cheerful trade. The photo on the left is of a 1926 model; below is the essentially unchanged swan boat of today.

25

Opposite: Quincy Market, *c.* 1900. Josiah Quincy, mayor of Boston from 1824-9, is often credited with transforming Boston from a small, colonial town into an important "modern" city. Among Quincy's accomplishments were the establishment of police and fire departments, public schools, and a new market fronting on historic Faneuil Hall. The cornerstone of the new market was laid on April 17, 1825, and the complex – known as the Quincy Market – opened for business just over a year later, replacing the old Fanueil Hall Market. Quincy Market, two storeys high, faced in granite, covering 27,000 square feet, met Boston's needs for well over 100 years, until the city's heavy traffic made a large in-town market impracticable. In the 1960s Boston's main market was relocated outside the city, and Quincy Market fell into decay. The complex was restored in the 1970s, as part of the Bicentennial Celebrations, and today Quincy Market is one of Boston's most popular shopping areas, where everything from books to bagels is sold by shops in the old market stalls.

Right: Although Quincy Market, like San Francisco's Ghiradelli Square, or London's Covent Garden Market, is no longer a living market, Boston still has active street markets. One of the liveliest is in Haymarket Square, where trucks and cars have taken the place of the horsecarts that once brought produce to Boston's first markets.

27

28

Fanueil Hall, as it looked in the 1920s (opposite) and appears today (below). The original building, designed by the painter John Smibert, was built in 1742 to house Boston's main market on its ground floor and the town meeting hall on its second floor. In 1806 the architect Charles Bulfinch added a third storey and a cupola with Fanueil Hall's distinctive weathervane, a gilded grasshopper, symbol of the Port of Boston.

Above right and left: Two contemporary views of the Quincy Market/Fanueil Hall Marketplace complex. The Quincy Market part of the complex consists of two warehouses flanking a central market. The architect, Alexander Parris, aimed to create an important civic monument: the main building was in Greek Revival style and incorporated a rotunda and massive cupola. The building's Doric columns were, in 1825, the largest single pieces of granite ever quarried in the United States. While the main building was granite, the flanking warehouses were brick and granite. In all, the central market had 108 stalls on the ground floor. Today, some 70 shops occupy the former stalls, and the warehouses also house shops and restaurants such as famed Durgin Park.

Just as the original Fanueil Hall market and meeting hall was an important landmark in eighteenth-century Boston, and the first Quincy Market was so in the nineteenth century, today's Quincy-Fanueil complex has contributed a good deal to the revitalization of downtown Boston. A neighborhood, which might have decayed after the central market relocated outside the city center in the 1970s, has become a vital part of the new Boston. Many young visitors who know nothing of the area's distinguished past now come to Boston specifically to visit its shops, restaurants, and bars. And probably few pause to consider how stalls selling souvlaki, pizza, or fish cakes recall a time when the surrounding neighborhoods really were all Greek, Italian, and Irish.

30

Above: Few scenes in Boston have changed less than this view of the Boston Public Library. One of Boston's great buildings, this Renaissance Revival library, designed by the New York firm of McKim, Mead, and White in 1895, stands beside a late-nineteenth century Italian Gothic church with a tall campanile and a characteristically Boston name: New Old South Church. In the background looms the new Prudential Center.

Opposite: This 1920s view of the Boston Public Library and the New Old South Church shows little difference in the look of the buildings, but much in the look of their surroundings. Modern Boston's lofty skyline may have made these once-imposing structures seem less impressive, but thoughtful landscaping has much enhanced their charm.

32

Opposite and right top: In mid-December 1891 history's first basketball game was played under the supervision of its inventor, Dr. James Naismith, in the gymnasium (photo right) of what is now Springfield College in Springfield, Massachusetts: the hoops the players used were old peach baskets nailed to the gym's balcony. By the turn of the century basketball had become an established sport (opposite), but the game was still a far cry from what it is today – note the sewn-closed hoop net and the absence of markings on the court floor, to say nothing of the uniforms.

Below: The Boston Garden, home of the Celtics. Dr. Naismith would have been amazed by what has become of the little game he invented to give his students wintertime exercise.

33

In 1885 Cornelius Vanderbilt II decided that he wanted a vacation get-away home and hired William Morris Hunt to design a suitable summer "cottage." The firm of landscape architect Frederick Law Olmsted was charged with laying out the extensive gardens. The result was The Breakers, the most opulent of the millionaires' cottages that line Cliff Walk in Newport, Rhode Island. Modeled on a Renaissance palace, the Breakers has some 70 rooms, of which the most spectacular is the two-storey Great Hall (below), with its rich marble decoration, broad sweeping staircase, and massive chandelier. Other rooms included a Music Room brought in its entirety from France, a Morning Room with allegorical paintings of the Muses, and the luxurious two-storey Dining Room. The *c.* 1900 photo on the right and the modern photo below it show that The Breakers remains impressively unchanged.

Newport's days of glory began after the Civil War, when some of America's richest families built "cottages" there. Mrs. William Astor's Newport ballroom held 400 dancers comfortably; this was the origin of the term "the 400." To be sure, most of those who came to Newport were of more modest means, and not a few had preceded the Astors: for years wealthy Southern families had vacationed there to escape the South's steamy summers. But after the Civil War, Newport's visitors increasingly came from New York and New England, lodging in the many small hotels and boarding houses that sprang up. Today, visitors still come to Newport to gape and the "cottages," most of which are now museums open to the public. The photos on this page show, clockwise from the top left: the Newport Casino in the 1890s; Newport beach *c.* 1920; and Newport today.

Mostly built during the nineteenth century, the handsome brick and stone railroad stations that dotted the Northeast were familiar to generations of commuters before being torn down in the 1950s and replaced by more anonymous structures. This Stamford, Connecticut, station illustrates the process: the 1934 photo above shows the old building; at the right, its modern successor.

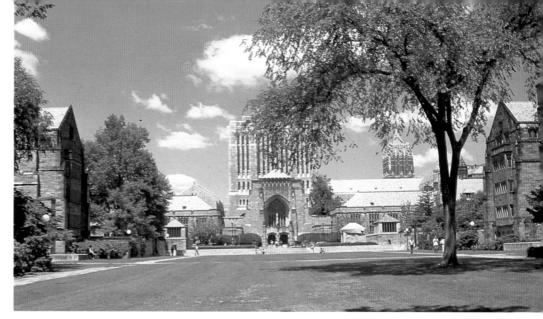

Founded in 1701, Yale University is the Northeast's second-oldest institution of higher education (Harvard, as its graduates never let Yalies forget, was founded 65 years earlier). Be that as it may, the first Ph.D.s in the country were awarded by Yale in 1861, only nine years before these students (left) in their splendid top-hats sat on "The Fence" for a commemorative photo. Today the top hats and The Fence are gone, and many of Yale's undergraduates are women (first admitted in 1969). Some of Yale's original red brick Georgian buildings still stand, along with a mix of later neo-Gothic structures such as Harkness Tower and recent additions by noted 20th-century architects such as Eero Saarinen and Philip Johnson: as the two contemporary photos above suggest, Yale's is one of the most architecturally diverse of the Ivy League campuses.

West Point, in New York's Hudson River Valley, was originally a strategic fort. Colonel Thaddeus Kosciusko, the Polish patriot who joined the colonists in their struggle against England, designed an elaborate system of fortifications along the Hudson, and in 1802 the most impressive of these became the new nation's first military academy. As the academy grew, many of its new buildings were finished in the neo-Gothic style, along with a scattering of Greek revival. Something of its present-day appearance is already evident in the turn-of-the-century photo on the upper right. Both Robert E. Lee and Ulysses S. Grant were West Point graduates, along with generals like John J. Pershing, president of the class of 1888 (right). In 1976, in a striking departure from tradition, West Point and the other service academies began to admit women, and today a significant percentage of the nearly 12,000 women who hold officer's commissions in the US Army are academy graduates.

Opposite top: Cadets on parade. Although the formal West Point marching uniform, with its brush-plumed shako (aka "tar bucket"), short-tailed tunic, and gleaming cross-straps, has changed slightly over the years, it is still based on a pattern dating from the early 1800s.

Opposite bottom: Cadets in undress uniform assemble for marching drill on the quad before Washington Hall.

The docks along the East River in New York City were nicknamed the "Street of Ships" in the mid-nineteenth century when the area was the center of shipping activity in one of the world's busiest ports. The South Street neighborhood, which enclosed some 11 blocks, was, as this 1860s photograph shows, a thicket of clipper ships and other blue-water craft tied up side by side, their jib-booms almost touching the warehouses that lined the quay. Yet in a few more years South Street would fall into decline, a victim of the technology of steam. The new steamships needed deeper water, leading to a steady shift in the development of docks and shipyards to the Hudson. Gradually the warehouses and countinghouses along South Street's Georgian-style dockside fell into decay, and by the 1950s many had either been torn down or were in danger of falling down. Of the older businesses in the area only the Fulton Fish Market continued to flourish. Yet a few of South Street's old architectural glories remained – mostly on Schermerhorn Row – and that was just as well, for help was at hand.

The entire South Street area might have been razed and this important chapter in New York City's history lost, had it not been for the growing preservation movement. By the 1980s plans were in place to preserve as much as possible of the old South Street neighborhood, both as a museum, and as a centerpiece for a revitalized neighborhood, with shops, restaurants, and a new Fulton Fish Market. The upper picture on the left shows the South Street Seaport as it appears today when viewed from the East River, and the lower picture is of one of its restored Georgian facades. In the upper picture, note also that in the background loom the twin towers of the World Trade Center, built between 1970 and 1977. Housing more than 350 companies, with some 50,000 employees, in two 110-storey-high towers, the Center represented a philosophy of urban revitalization opposite to that of the Seaport, for to make way for the Center old neighborhoods were not preserved, but obliterated. In March 1993 the Center was the subject of international headlines when it was severely damaged by a terrorist bomb.

42

The building of the Brooklyn Bridge between Manhattan and Brooklyn is one of the great sagas of American engineering history. The 1,595-foot suspension bridge – the longest ever built when it opened – was of a startlingly novel design by a brilliant engineer named John Roebling. Injured in an accident at the bridge site, Roebling died when his intended masterpiece was hardly begun. Roebling's relatively inexperienced son, Washington, saw the project through to completion, despite chronic ill-health which largely prevented him from visiting the site. When the bridge opened on May 24, 1883, some 150,000 New Yorkers became the first to view the sweeping panorama of Manhattan from the bridge. Celebrated by Hart Crane and Walt Whitman, the bridge is one of New York's most enduring monuments. The picture opposite is of the bridge during construction in 1878; that on the left shows it against the skyline of 1916; and the lower pictures are contemporary views.

44

Streets like Orchard and Hester Streets in New York's Lower East Side were bustling open-air markets in the 1890s (left), the 1920s (opposite) – and still are today (below and lower left). Fashions have changed, and now more novelties than necessities are sold, but the Lower East Side is still a favorite destination for bargain seekers.

In the nineteenth and early twentieth centuries, the Lower East Side, celebrated in such films as *Hester Street*, was a largely Jewish neighborhood, as immigrants from Eastern Europe and Russia poured through Ellis Island into New York. Today, new waves of immigrants from the Far East and Latin America have added their distinctive cultures to the neighborhood.

New York's Fifth Avenue, one of the most famous streets in America, is also the site of several of its most famous buildings. The Empire State building has probably been New York City's best-known symbol ever since it was built by the architectural firm of Shreve, Lamb, and Harmon in 1931. Nearly as famous are the massive rectangular towers of Rockefeller Center, still a-building in the mid-1930s photo opposite, which looks down the avenue from 58th Street to the Empire State Building. Fifth Avenue itself was laid out in 1824 to be the focal point of a new residential district in Manhattan, and by the turn of the century much of the avenue was indeed lined with elegant brownstone mansions. Many of the wealthy who built summer "cottages" in Newport, Rhode Island, had their New York townhouses on Fifth Avenue. To the east, Park and Lexington Avenues paralleled Fifth Avenue, and were developed as Fifth Avenue began to fill up. Cross-streets running east from Fifth Avenue, from about 58th Street into the 90s, still have some of the city's finest turn-of-the-century buildings, including two by Stanford White in one block alone: the Metropolitan Club and the Harmonie Club on East 60th Street. And Fifth Avenue itself is lined with some of New York's finest hotels, including the Pierre and the Sherry Netherland, its best-known museum, the Metropolitan Museum of Art, and its most famous park, Central Park. In this photo yet another of Fifth Avenue's landmarks is just visible on the left: the gothic spires of Saint Patrick's Cathedral.

Taken from essentially the same perspective as the photo opposite, the modern photo on the left shows Fifth Avenue today. The degree to which the city built upwards in the intervening 60 years is all too evident, yet much remains as before: St Pat's, Rockefeller Center, and, of course, the Empire State Building, still upper Fifth Avenue's southern lynchpin, its majesty unaffected by the imposing twin towers of the World Trade Center that loom in the remote distance. Although the 102-storey Empire State is no longer America's tallest building (it is No. 3), it is still unique – what other building would a self-respecting King Kong have wanted to climb? With its 203-foot TV antenna, the building is a total of 1,453 feet tall and has 73 elevators, and five acres of windows. Anyone who doesn't want to take one of the elevators can climb the building's 1,860 steps, pausing to rest at the observation decks on the 86th and 102nd floors.

48

By 1879 New York's Catholics were sufficiently numerous and prosperous to decide that their cathedral church, Saint Patrick's, was insufficiently grand. The old St. Pat's had been built, in the Gothic Revival style, in 1815, at Mott, Prince, and Mulberry Streets, not far from the Bowry. The new Saint Patrick's Cathedral on Fifth Avenue at 50th and 51st Streets took more than 50 years to build: it was begun in 1858, dedicated in 1879, but not finished until 1906. At that time the East 60s were *the* place to live in New York, and many of Saint Patrick's parishioners feared that their cathedral might still be too far south. But as the city developed, Saint Patrick's found itself in a prime, central location. By the 1920s (far left), open-topped double decker buses, flotillas of taxis, and ever more private cars were streaming up and down busy Fifth Avenue. In another 50 years the traffic would be so heavy that major streets like Fifth Avenue had to be made one-way. By then, Saint Patrick's 330-foot towers were no longer the tallest points in the neighborhood: the Tishman Building rose to 39 stories, the Olympic Towers went to 51 stories, and twin skyscrapers at 650 and 666 Fifth Avenue dwarfed Saint Patrick's (left). Some old neighbors remain near Saint Patrick's: the jeweler Cartier still occupies the handsome 1905 town house that was converted into a shop in 1917. And three of New York's best-known stores, Saks Fifth Avenue, Tiffany and Bonwit Teller, have been there since the 1930s.

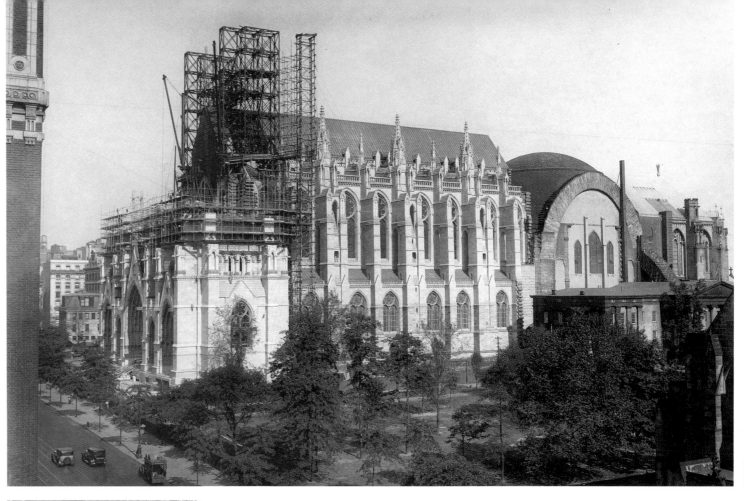

Above and left: It took almost 50 years to build Saint Patrick's cathedral, but the Episcopalian cathedral church of Saint John the Divine on Amsterdam Avenue was begun in 1892 and still isn't finished. The cathedral was meant to be the largest church in America, and boasts that it is the largest Gothic cathedral in the world, with seating for 10,000. It is Gothic only in a sense, for it began as a Byzantine-Romanesque church; when the first architects died in 1911, the commission was handed to Ralph Adams Cram, who continued it in the Gothic style. The upper photo is from 1930, when work on the towers was beginning; the modern photo, left, shows detail of the Gothic buttresses and the 320-foot Byzantine transcept.

Two views of Manhattan's ever-changing face. The photos on the left and left below show Fifth Avenue at 60th Street, as it looked at the turn of the century and as it looks today: the sometime mansion on the northeast corner is now the Metropolitan Club. The 1923 photo opposite is of Fifth Avenue and 57th Street, as is the modern picture below.

Fifth Av. Police Tower. B. 42533. Copyright 1923. by Irving Underhill N.Y.C

Times Square, looking south, on election eve in 1948 (right) and today (right below). Almost every visitor to New York makes a bee-line for Times Square, only to discover that the city's most famous square is really a triangle, formed by the confluence of Broadway and Seventh Avenue. The area, originally known as Longacre Square, contained many of the city's stables. In 1904 the New York *Times* moved into the neighborhood and established its headquarters in the triangular building built for it by the firm of Eidlitz and MacKenzie at One Times Square. After the *Times* moved to quarters just off Times Square on West 43rd Street, extensive remodeling in the 1960s stripped the original building of much of its character. Times Square itself was New York's first great theater district, home of the original Metropolitan Opera House, built in 1883. The theaters attracted hotels and restaurants, and until fairly recently the area remained one of New York's most exciting neighborhoods. But for at least the past quarter-century Times Square has become ever less glamorous, and so far, plans for its revival have made small headway.

Opposite left: Times Square as it appeared in 1952; pedestrians are standing, uncharacteristically, on the curb, waiting out an air raid drill. At that time the square still retained many of its storied landmarks, such as the *Times* Building, the old Astor Hotel, and various splendid first-run picture palaces.

Opposite right: Times Square today has lost much of its old personality. Now it has few grandiose pretensions, and some of what was once charmingly raffish about it has drifted into mere seediness or worse.

54

It's a long way from R.H. Macy's first Dry Goods emporium (far left) to today's enormous store which covers 2,151,000 square feet on another of New York's triangular squares: like Times Square, Herald Square, at Broadway and Sixth Avenue, was named for a newspaper, the New York *Herald*, now the *International Herald Tribune*. Also once located on Herald Square was Macy's greatest rival, Gimbel's, now only a memory.

New York's great department stores drew enormous crowds of Christmas shoppers from the 1940s (top left) through the 70s, when self-service discount stores began to undercut their business substantially. A number of majestic old stores closed, including such long-standing institutions as Best and Company and B. Altman. Those that remained were forced to cut back on staff and service in an attempt to become more competitive.

One of New York's great pastimes, whether in the 1930s (below left) or today (above) is window-shopping. The major department stores go all-out with their window displays at Christmas. Certainly more tourists visit Manhattan to see the Christmas window displays than to attend the theater and visit museums, but then that is probably equally the case at all other times of year as well.

Not only is New York famous for "squares" that are triangular, one of its most famous buildings is also triangular: the Flatiron Building at Fifth Avenue, Broadway and 23rd Street, aka Madison Square. The picture above shows Madison Square in 1885, some 17 years before the Flatiron Building was erected. This was a time when people could still ride on horseback over Manhattan's cobblestones.

Above right: The Flatiron Building under construction. Completed in 1902, its unusual shape not only answered the problem of its awkward site with great imagination, its sheer height – 286 feet – delighted New Yorkers, who were becoming fascinated by the idea of skyscrapers. Finally, its facade, rich in French Renaissance detail, was a model of restrained elegance.

FULLER BUILDING B-19866
Flatiron Bldg.
Broadway & 5th Ave.
Copyright 1912 By
IRVING UNDERHILL, N.Y.

Two views of the finished Flatiron Building (Fuller Building): one (left) from 1912, and the other (above) contemporary. The building's site, Madison Square, was in fact at one time the home of the original Madison Square Garden sports arena. It is also the setting in which what is reputed to have been America's first baseball team played its games in 1842.

Opposite: Two views of Wall Street, looking west: the left-hand photo was taken in 1894; the right-hand, in 1992. Both show, on the right, the steps of the Subtreasury Building, with its statue of George Washington, and, at the end of the street, Trinity Church. Little else, however, remains unchanged. The "wall" in the Wall Street, incidentally, refers to a wooden palisade built there by Peter Stuyvesant in 1653 as a protection against Indian and English raids.

This page: The speed with which New York's skyline changes is well illustrated by these views of lower Manhattan taken from the Battery. The upper picture is not really old – 1951 – but the difference between it and the contemporary picture below is enormous, the World Trade Center's huge twin towers being only the most obvious element of change. What has not changed is the Staten Island Ferry: it still charges only a pittance for spectacular views of both the city and the Statue of Liberty.

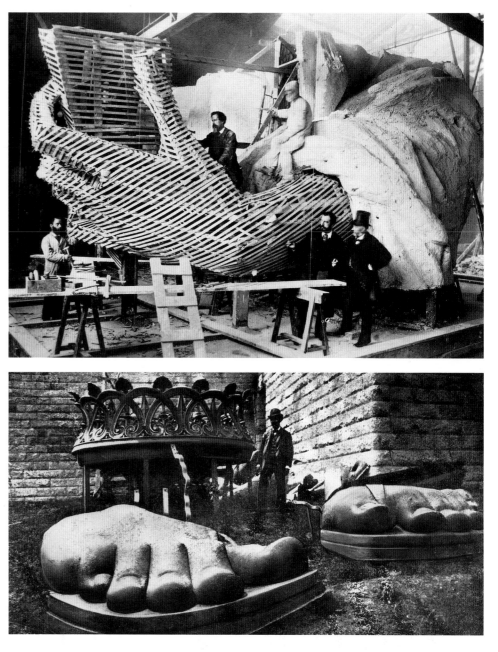

60

The American writer O. Henry once said that the Statue of Liberty was given to the American people by the French nation in 1886 to welcome "Irish immigrants to the Dutch city of New York."

The statue was, of course, a gift to commemorate a friendship dating back to the Revolutionary War, when the Marquis de Lafayette and other Frenchmen joined the Americans in their struggle for freedom from England.

Fund-raising for the statue was led by Ferdinand de Lesseps, builder of the Suez Canal, assisted by Gustave Eiffel, later architect of the Eiffel Tower. More than $400,000 was raised, and the sculptor F. A. Bartholdi began work on the huge figure in 1875.

After its unveiling in 1884, the statue was dismantled, packed in 214 crates, and shipped across the Atlantic to the US, where it was reassembled. The statue's great torch was finally lit at the official dedication on October 28, 1886.

The seven points in the statue's crown symbolize liberty beaming forth to each of the seven continents. In her left hand the massive 151-foot figure holds a tablet inscribed with the Declaration of Independence; in her right, the liberty torch.

Inscribed on the base of the statue is the famous poem written by Emma Lazarus in 1883 in which the Liberty, speaking for America, welcomes all oppressed immigrants, the "huddled masses yearning to breathe free."

The Statue of Liberty is still an inspiring sight, especially at night, when its crown and torch are illuminated and the statue stands out dramatically against the lower-Manhattan skyline.

The federal government opened Ellis Island as a processing center for immigrants in 1892; a fanciful brick and limestone building with turrets was built in 1900 after a fire destroyed the original reception center. About a million immigrants were entering the US each year when the photo of the reception center opposite, bottom, was taken in 1912. The admission process was long and tedious, and new immigrants spent many hours in the massive Registry Hall (near left, below), which held 5000, waiting to be called for physical exams and document checks. Some left the hall with new names when exasperated immigrations officials were unable to spell the immigrants' multisyllabic real names. But to most, the delays and aggravations were an acceptable price for at last being able, like the family shown opposite, top, to stand on the Ellis Island dock, waiting for the ferry that would take them to their new home. Legislation gradually limited imigration from southern and eastern Europe, and by the 1950s, the cavernous Registry Hall often stood empty. Ellis Island was finally closed as a processing center in 1954, but in 1965 it was declared a National Monument, joined with the Statue of Liberty National Monument, and is now a museum of immigration (color photos top left and far left).

63

Opposite and left: Atlantic City was one of the country's first great resorts: the United States Hotel, with 600 rooms, was the largest in the country when it was built there in 1854, and the Marlborough-Blenheim was the first to have a private bath with every room. These turn-of-the-century photos show how the town's famous five-mile Boardwalk and Steel Pier attracted day-trippers who came to stroll by the sea.

Below left and right: Atlantic City's sedately-dressed visitors of yore might be shocked if they could see their modern counterparts in shorts, sneakers, and T-shirts. And they might be even more dismayed if they could see the photo below of the destruction of the once-elegant Blenheim Hotel in 1979. As to their opinion of Atlantic City's current incarnation as a kind of junior Las Vegas, it is probably best not to speculate.

65

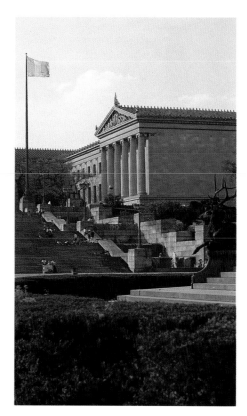

Left: There are many famous buildings in the historic square-mile that forms the heart of old Philadelphia, but probably none more so than Independence Hall, where the Declaration of Independence was signed in 1776. It is a favored site for patriotic celebrations, and these pictures show two variations on one such event. The upper shows a crowd – somehow rather "small-town" in aspect – gathered before the Hall in 1937 to observe the 150th anniversary of the Constitution. The lower photo, also taken at Independence Hall, is of the Constitution's "show-biz"-like 200th-anniversary celebration in 1987.

Right and Opposite: The picture opposite shows a 1938 view of Philadelphia, looking from the Art Museum down Benjamin Franklin Parkway towards City Hall. The lower right photo is of the same vista in 1990, showing both skyline changes and the new, controversial "Rocky" statue on the Art Museum grounds. The upper right picture shows the imposing museum itself; its classical facade dates from 1876.

Pittsburgh, with its superb triangular site where the Allegheny and Monongahela Rivers meet to form the Ohio, was first important as a "Gateway to the West." Then coal, iron, and steel made Pittsburgh even important. By the end of the Civil War one half of the nation's iron was made there, and by the turn of the century Andrew Carnegie had made Pittsburgh the steel capital of the world. By the 1940s (opposite) Pittsburgh had one of the most severe pollution problems in the country. Well into the 1960s the Pittsburgh sky was almost perpetually dark and smoggy, ultimately forcing the city to undertake a concerted campaign to clean up its air. At the same time, many landmark Pittsburg buildings were torn down in a frenzy of urban renewal. Today Pittsburgh is one of the most liveable cities in the Northeast, with clean air, a revitalized down-town business district, and even a scattering of nineteenth-century buildings that escaped the urban renewal movement. At Point State Park, a 150-foot fountain commemorates the site where Pittsburgh first began at the confluence of the rivers.

THE SOUTH

Between 1763 and 1767 two Englishmen, Charles Mason and Jeremiah Dixon, surveyed the disputed borders between Pennsylvania, Maryland, and northern Virginia (today's state of West Virginia). What soon came to be known as the Mason-Dixon line took on added importance 100 years later, when the slave states south of the Mason-Dixon line stood against the free states to the North. Even today the Mason-Dixon line is the symbolic northern boundary of the Old South, the "Land of Dixie," where the nation's first plantations made cotton king. Cotton and tobacco are still important crops in the South, and Southern hospitality is still legendary, but today's South is more focused on its hopes for the future than on memories of the past.

Even though Virginia lies along the northern reaches of America's South, it has long been at the heart of the South's political, cultural, and economic life. "The Old Dominion," as Virginia was known, was originally so large that eight states were carved from its vast expanse. The nation's first permanent English settlement was established there, at Jamestown, Virginia, in 1607. The country's first African-Americans arrived there in 1619, some as indentured servants but others as the first of the thousands of slaves who would be brought to the South to work the land. Seven of the country's first 12 presidents came from Virginia, first of America's Thirteen Colonies. And, of course, the capital of the Confederacy was there, in Richmond.

Although English settlers first colonized Virginia, and their descendants pushed the frontier west into Kentucky and Tennessee, Spanish and French explorers had already been active elsewhere in the South. The Spanish opened up Florida, founding America's first permanent settlement in 1565 at Saint Augustine. Florida passed permanently from the Spanish to the United States only in 1819, so it is not surprising that the old quarters of towns like Saint Augustine and Pensacola retain a distinctive Spanish flavor.

Although the Spanish held Louisiana between 1762 and 1801, it was the French who left the most lasting impression there, most famously in "le Vieux Carré" (The French Quarter) of New Orleans. Houses with elaborate wrought-iron balconies line the French Quarter's narrow streets, and restaurants serve up French and Creole specialities to the thousands of tourists who flock there each year for Mardi Gras.

Although its settlement by colonists from England, Spain, and France meant that the South as a whole had a diverse heritage, one factor tied the region together: slavery, sometimes called by Southerners "Our Peculiar Institution." Slave labor supported the South's vast tobacco and cotton plantations, allowing generations of white Southerners to make a fine living from the land. Today many ante-bellum estates, from George Washington's Mount Vernon and Thomas Jefferson's Monticello to the grand mansions on the Mississippi, preserve a sense of what life was like in the era commemorated in the novel and film *Gone With the Wind*.

Left: In the early 1920s the elegant Miami Beach Bath Club served lunch to its members at New York prices. They could well afford to pay. "The Beach" had been reclaimed from 1,600 acres of mangrove swamp, only a few years before, by planter John S. Collins and financier Carl F. Fisher. The new resort rivaled staid Palm Beach, up the coast, as a fashionable watering hole for wealthy expatriates from the freezing north.

Opposite: Through decades of boom and bust, Miami Beach has retained the vitality of its halcyon days as a winter resort. Colorfully dressed tourists mingle comfortably with retirees in the city's Art Deco Historic District, where pierced and patterned masonry and pastel sidewalks recall the boom-time 1930s. The developers wanted new-looking buildings, in the style of the 1925 Paris Exposition des Arts Décoratifs, and Art Deco came to Collins Avenue to stay.

During the first half of the nineteenth century, as the industrial revolution began to transform the Northeast, and as settlers pushed the frontier farther and farther west, the South remained relatively unchanged: Southern cities such as Richmond, Virginia, Charleston, South Carolina, Atlanta, Georgia – even Washington, D.C., the nation's capital – were small by Northern standards. When General William Tecumsah Sherman burned Atlanta, the city had a population of a mere 10,000. Astonishingly, Atlanta doubled its size in the five years after the Civil War ended. The reason: Northern businesses in search of cheap labor relocated there – a foretaste of what would happen elsewhere in the South in our own time.

Ravaged by the Civil War, exploited by Northern interests during Reconstruction, the South lagged behind much of the rest of the country in prosperity in the late nineteenth and early twentieth centuries. For a while, the rich coal fields of Appalachia brought wealth into that region, but the production of cheap electricity by the TVA put an end to the boom, and although the TVA brought a measure of prosperity to the rest of the region, Appalachia has remained a synonym for poverty and despair to this day.

Prosperity began to return to the South in earnest in the 1960s, with cities in the so-called "research triangle" – Raleigh, Durham and Chapel Hill, and Atlanta – becoming symbols of the "new" South. Atlanta boasted the first skyscraper in the Southeast to top 40 stories – on old Peachtree Street. The 1960s also saw the Civil Rights struggle, which emerged in the South and spread across the entire nation. Until the election of Bill Clinton, most Americans thought of Little Rock, Arkansas, mainly as the site of the confrontation at the Little Rock High School in 1957 during the struggle over school desegregation. Yet today cities like Little Rock and Atlanta are home to a prosperous African-American middle class.

Florida, the South's most densely populated and fastest growing state, is perhaps the quintessential tourist state: Disneyland and the myriad attractions of Orlando attract millions of visitors every year. Refugees from Cuba have made Miami into a city where Spanish is spoken as readily as English. Other kinds of refugees, retirees fleeing harsh Northern winters, are colonizing much of west Florida. In some Florida settlements, such as Englewood, the oldest building in town was built in the 1950s, and most of the town went up in the 1980s.

In a sense, the South's best symbol of the complex interaction of change and continuity is to be found at 1600 Pennsylvania Avenue in Washington, D.C.: the White House. George Washington laid the cornerstone there in 1792, and every president since John Adams has lived there. Under President Harry Truman the whole of the interior of the building was gutted and rebuilt, yet like the South itself, the White House still maintains much of its original facade almost unchanged, masking the impressive change within.

Opposite: Half a century ago, the steeple of Saint Michael's Episcopal Church was one of Charleston's oldest landmarks. It soared 182 feet over the palmetto trees and historic buildings of Broad and Meeting Streets. Built between 1752 and 1761, St. Michael's, the city's oldest surviving church, bears a close resemblance to London's Saint Martin-in-the-Fields and may even have been designed by the same architect, James Gibbs. Its four-faced clock was installed in 1764, and the steeple was long a beacon for mariners. George Washington and Robert E. Lee both worshipped here on visits to the port.

Right: When Hurricane Hugo swept through Charleston in September 1989, one of the city's greatest losses was the steeple of St. Michael's. But Charlestonians lost no time in restoring this cherished landmark. They are used to the tropical storms that have roared up from the Caribbean since the city was founded on its peninsula more than 200 years ago. In fact, civic pride is such that the site is referred to as "the place where the Ashley and Cooper Rivers meet to form the Atlantic Ocean."

75

Opposite: Before the vast urban renewal project undertaken in the 1950s, the historic port of Baltimore, Maryland, had changed little over the years. Founded on the Patapsco River in 1729, the city grew rapidly as an international port on Chesapeake Bay. Its first two streets, Baltimore and Charles, cross just north of the harbor, and downtown Baltimore grew up around this intersection. Here were the courthouse, city hall, and the main financial section. Along the waterfront, shipyards, refineries, factories, and freight yards made the city a major commercial center. Shipping was dominated by powerful concerns like the United Fruit Company, which grew tropical crops in Latin America for transport north.

Left: Today Baltimore's skyline is dramatically changed by the renovation that began in the 1950s and is still going on. The 22-acre Charles Center project brought streamlined new office buildings and city parks to the downtown area. Landmarks like the Washington Monument in Mount Vernon Place and Johns Hopkins University coexist with gleaming skyscrapers, hotels, and galleries. The revitalized port area has become a major tourist attraction and a source of civic pride. Much has gone on here since Baltimore first launched its famous clipper ships, renowned for their missions of "deviltry and speed," like rum-running from Barbados.

Top left: The nation's Capitol as seen in an 1860 photograph by Mathew Brady. The original building, burned by the British during the War of 1812, was rebuilt by architects Benjamin Latrobe and, after 1817, Charles Bulfinch. Between 1851 and 1863 wings were added and the dome was enlarged by Thomas U. Walter, as can be seen here.

Above: The first inauguration of Abraham Lincoln on the steps of the Capitol, still under renovation, on March 4, 1861.

Top right: President John F. Kennedy takes the oath of office, administered by Chief Justice Earl Warren, on January 20, 1961.

Right: The Capitol resplendent with flags and banners for the inauguration of Bill Clinton on January 20, 1993. It was the most expensive inaugural ever.

Above: The Capitol dome crowns what was once called Jenkins Hill, now Capitol Hill – the point where the four quadrants of the city converge. French major Pierre Charles L'Enfant, engaged to plan the new Federal City by George Washington, reported to him in 1791: "I could discover no one [site] so advantageously to greet the congressional building as is that on the West End of Jenkins Heights, which stands as a pedestal waiting for a monument."

Right: The Grand Review of Union Armies along the Mall, which extends from the foot of Capitol Hill to the present-day Lincoln Memorial. This photograph was taken on May 24, 1865, six weeks after the Confederate surrender at Appomattox Court House and 39 days after the assassination of Lincoln.

Servicemen and women of World War II
head up a skating party on the frozen
reflecting pool before the Lincoln
Memorial. The sailors in this 1943
photograph are U.S. Navy yeomen; the
women are officers of the British Women's
Royal Navy Service (WRNS).

Top left: The serene grandeur of the Lincoln Memorial today, more than 70 years after its dedication. The structure was designed by Henry Bacon in 1922. Twenty years before, there had been vigorous debate in Congress about its location on land reclaimed from the Potomac. Speaker of the House Joe Cannon of Illinois asserted roundly that "I'll never let a memorial to Abraham Lincoln be erected in that god-damned swamp." But Cannon was outvoted, and the memorial was constructed on fill. Its architect was honored in the naming of block-long Henry Bacon Drive, which slants off Constitution Avenue between 21st and 23rd Streets NW.

79

Far left: The temporary buildings (tempos) erected for the War and Navy Departments during World War II lined both sides of the Lincoln Memorial reflecting pool, which was bridged to connect the buildings. This 1942 photograph was taken from the Washington Monument shortly before pictures from that vantage point were banned for security reasons. The unsightly bridges across the Mall and the reflecting pool were dismantled soon after the war, but the last tempo survived until 1973.

Left: The imposing statue of Lincoln inside the memorial is the work of sculptor Daniel Chester French, who also has a Washington street named for him. Dedicated with the building in 1922, the statue has recently been cleaned and restored to its original state. This monument to the best-loved statesman in our history is a shrine for Americans and visitors from other countries alike.

Landmark aircraft in the history of U.S. aviation (left, top) are now on display in the National Air and Space Museum of the Smithsonian Institution. This is one of Washington's foremost attractions and the most-visited museum in the world. Opened in 1976, it occupies the site of the old District of Columbia Armory, which was a Civil War hospital during the 1860s. The Wright brothers' plane hangs over the former center of the Armory complex, which was demolished in 1964. The museum is on the north side of Independence Avenue, opposite 6th Street SW, which once crossed the Mall.

For many years, Linbergh's *Spirit of St. Louis* hung over the main entrance to the Smithsonian's Arts and Industries Building (left below). This 1928 photo shows the entrance hall to the National Museum Building, as it was named in 1876, when it was built as an annex to the Castle to accommodate the Institution's fast-growing collection. Affectionately known as "the nation's attic," the Smithsonian has so many artifacts and works of art that thousands of them have never even been displayed. The Arts and Industries Building is more than two acres in extent. It was built in 1875-6 at a cost of $310,000 – a bargain price for a government building, even in those days. Originally, the museum exhibited industrial, technical, and ethnographic collections related to national resources and contemporary views on human progress.

"The Castle" (left, top) in an 1860s photograph by Mathew Brady. The Smithsonian Institution was created by Congress in 1846, when Englishman James Smithson left a bequest of more than half a million dollars to the United States to "found at Washington, under the name of the Smithsonian Institution, an establishment for the increase and diffusion of knowledge." The Norman-style building was designed by New York architect James Renwick, Jr., and built on the south side of the Mall. Completed in 1856, it contained a lecture hall, museum, art gallery, library, laboratories, office, and living quarters for the director. Instruments in the museum's towers were used to monitor the weather. The Castle is still the Institution's headquarters and symbol, and one of Washington's favorite landmarks. Behind the Castle the Smithsonian's extensive gardens (far left, below) beautify the site and preserve the nation's horticultural heritage. During the 1860s, many of the museum's agricultural specimens were turned over to the newly-created Department of Agriculture, whose headquarters was aligned with the Castle.

Left: A 75-foot dinosaur is patiently reconstructed by Smithsonian workers in 1931 for display in the museum's great exhibit hall.

Above: Arlington National Cemetery, Virginia, 1926: a dedication of the memorial to chaplains of every faith who died in World War I, then known as "The Great World War."

Right: Construction of the Tomb of the Unknown Soldier underway at Arlington in 1931. The 10-ton marble slab for the 50-ton tomb is in place, and a permanent vigil is maintained by sentries to this day.

Above: The "Great World War" section of Arlington National Cemetery as it looked in the 1930s. More than 175,000 servicemen and women from every major conflict are interred at Arlington.

Left: Honor guard at the Tomb of the Unknown Soldier during a Memorial Day observance. The national cemetery now has monuments to "the Unknowns" of all the major service branches.

84

Opposite: a view of historic Broad Street, Charleston, South Carolina, in the late 1920s. Originally called Cooper Street, after one of the province's Lord Proprietors, the thoroughfare gained its present name because it was the city's widest street. During the 1920s trolley cars carried local passenger traffic past the three- and four-story buildings of the financial district. Trade was the port's lifeblood from its beginnings in 1670.

Right: This contemporary view shows the faithful preservation of Broad Street's buildings, characterized by design elements adapted from the British colony of Barbados because of Charleston's sultry climate. Multistory balconies and piazzas allowed cool air to circulate. The distinctive palmetto tree, with its fanlike foliage, is emblematic of Charleston. In the distance is St. Michael's Episcopal Church, the city's oldest surviving house of worship.

Left: Stately Broad Street proceeds to Meeting Street and the Charleston County Courthouse. This intersection is called the Four Corners of Law, because four kinds of law are represented in its buildings: county, federal (the U.S. Courthouse), municipal (City Hall), and religious (St. Michael's).

The famous resort of Hot Springs, Arkansas, in 1935, (above) showing Central Avenue, the main thoroughfare, with its elegant Bathhouse Row. The Ozarks' spa grew rapidly during the late nineteenth century, when the fame of its pristine spring water, believed to have curative properties, drew thousands to the region. Some of them stayed to incorporate the city of Hot Springs in 1851. Completion of the railroad in 1874 made travel through the rugged Ozarks easier and attracted famous visitors, including Jay Gould, Andrew Carnegie, and Theodore Roosevelt.

Opposite below: Arkansas' foremost city, Hot Springs today is the center of a 5,839-acre national park that takes in part of the wooded mountains that encircle the city. Most of the hot springs that were eventually capped and channeled to Bathhouse Row still flow, but only the Buckstaff Bathhouse still offers baths to the public. Landmarks here include the 16-storey, Art Deco Medical Arts Building, which was for many years the tallest in the state.

Above is the busy railroad depot at Eureka Springs, Arkansas, in the late 1800s. News of the "Indian Healing Spring" at this site attracted both visitors and settlers, who established the lively resort town in 1880. Dozens of boardinghouses and, eventually, grand hotels, sprang up here at the turn of the century. Today part of the Eureka Springs Historic District, the depot (left) displays equipment that brought the first rail travelers to the great resort in 1883.

Above: A panoramic view of Atlanta, Georgia, during the Civil War. On the right is Peachtree Street.

Opposite: Peachtree Street and Atlanta's ravaged rail lines, the primary cause of the city's destruction by Sherman's Army.

Left: Modern Atlanta's gleaming skyline includes more than two dozen skyscrapers housing one of the nation's most vital financial centers. The gilded dome of the state capitol has been a landmark since 1889.

Far left: Colorful Peachtree Fountain Plaza, a gathering place in the best tradition of old and new Atlanta.

Stone Mountain, Georgia, (above) is just that – the world's largest piece of exposed granite. This 1923 photograph shows the beginning of the gigantic monument that would take shape here over the next 47 years. In the foreground is the lamp house that projected the images of the three mounted Confederate heroes onto the face of the rock.

At the right is the relief sculpture of Confederate statesman Jefferson Davis and Generals Robert E. Lee and Thomas "Stonewall" Jackson, completed in 1970. Three sculptors, beginning with Gutzon Borglum of Mount Rushmore fame, spent more than 50 years creating the monument.

Above is a detail of the 90- by 190-foot carving at Stone Mountain Park, the world's largest bas-relief sculpture.

Above: Sharecroppers pick cotton in the Deep South in the 1920s. This crop had been the cornerstone of the South's agrarian economy, surpassing tobacco, sugar cane, and rice – all equally labor-intensive commodities – since before the Civil War: in 1859 alone the South produced 5.3 million bales.

Above: A huge modern combine performs the once back-breaking task of harvesting cotton in a field at Tyronza, Arkansas. Machinery became inseparable from cotton production with Eli Whitney's invention of the cotton gin in 1793.

Left: Florida's vast agricultural industry concentrates on citrus crops and vegetables, as on this farm near Homestead, where migrant workers tend the fields. The state's mild climate makes year-round production possible.

92

Right: Savannah as a Confederate naval center during the Civil War. Its location on Georgia's Atlantic coastal plain, with access to the inland by river, had made it a major port soon after its foundation in 1733. It's Cotton Exchange was the world's center for trading the commodity before the Civil War. During the conflict, Savannah was blockaded by the Union navy and finally encircled by Sherman's army. The city surrendered peacefully on December 22, 1864, and was spared the destruction suffered by Atlanta.

Top left: Savannah's historic River Street is on the eastern edge of the downtown waterfront, along the Savannah River. The city's maritime glory days are recalled by the Ships of the Sea Museum, with its big collection of ship models, paintings, and other mementoes. The world's first transatlantic steamship was named for Savannah.

Left: Gracious Riverfront Plaza is one of Savannah's many historic districts, including the two-and-a-half-square-mile tract encompassing all of the original city plan. Filled with parks and plazas, Savannah has more than 5,000 oak trees along its principal streets. It is the fastest-growing port on the South Atlantic coast.

94

Left: The broad, hard-packed sand beaches of Daytona Beach made it one of Florida's earliest resorts, congenial to sun seekers and auto racers alike. This is more true than ever now that the Daytona International Speedway has made the city a mecca for professional racers. Photographed from Sunglow Fishing Pier at Daytona Beach Shores, this panoramic view shows the many hotels that have sprung up here in the last 30 years, attracting thousands of tourists, including college students on spring vacation.

Above: A far less populous Daytona Beach during the 1920s, when wealthy tourists tested the speed of their vehicles on the 500-foot-wide strip of sand. Automobile companies, too, brought new models here for tryouts. By this time, the city named for Mathias Day, an immigrant from Ohio, was already some 50 years old. Like nearby Ormond Beach, Daytona was part of the resort empire created by hotel-and-railroad builder Henry M. Flagler, during the late 1900s.

Left: Tourists of the 1930s, seemingly unaffected by the Great Depression, enjoy tropical Daytona. Before the resort-building boom of the 1880s, this area was known for its wealthy sugar plantations. Originally, it was the home of the Timucuan Indians.

Inimitable Miami, and offshore Miami Beach, in some of their many guises: Above, Miami by moonlight, sparkling with vitality on the shores of Biscayne Bay. Right, an orange juice vendor on Biscayne Boulevard supplies a fashionable customer during the 1920s. By this time, Miami had a population of 30,000 – up from 1,500 in 1896, thanks largely to the arrival of Flagler's railroad. The population would triple by 1926, during the decade's great real-estate boom.

Above: Hot dog vendors never looked as good as they do today in – where else? – extravagant Miami Beach.

Near right above: Luxurious Miami Beach curves away into the distance: shoulder-to-shoulder hotels and resorts, mansions and waterways, pools, and deep-green tropical parks. Wrested from the mangroves and water moccasins by entrepreneur Carl Fisher during the 1920s, "the Beach" has never looked back, despite the vicissitudes of hard times, hurricanes, and the rapid rise of the central-Florida resorts centered on the Walt Disney Vacation World complex at Orlando.

Above: Miami Beach's recently-restored South Beach, its waters dotted with colorful pleasure boats, is thronged with people who wouldn't be anywhere else.

Left: The almost rustic Miami Beach on which these 1920s belles take the sun seems a world away from the frenetic scene today.

THE MIDWEST

The Midwest often boasts of being the "heartland of America" – perhaps, in so far as the phrase has a cultural connotation, in reaction to the condescension of residents of certain other parts of America, particularly those who dwell on the Atlantic or Pacific coasts (and seem to think of the Midwest as a place over which to fly). But there is certainly no denying that the Midwest is America's geographic heartland, an immense region that stretches from the Allegheney Mountains of Pennsylvania to the Rocky Mountains, and from the border of Canada to the borders of the South and Southwest. It includes no less than 12 large states: Illinois, Indiana, Iowa, Kansas, Michigan, Minnesota, Missouri, Nebraska, North Dakota, Ohio, South Dakota, and Wisconsin.

Between the bracketing mountains stretch mile upon mile of the fertile plains that symbolize the region; not surprisingly, a number of the Midwestern states' official seals show fields of grain and sheaves of wheat. Yet the Midwest is more than plain and prairies: the glacial hills and valleys of Wisconsin, Minnesota, and Michigan are home to vast forests and are dotted with countless lakes. Along the northeast shoulder of the Midwest are the Great Lakes, bordered by some of the country's most important industrial cities, most especially Chicago, the largest inland port in the world and now the third largest city in the United States. Along its southern edge, much of the Midwest shares mountainous borders with the South.

During the first centuries of what would become the United States, the territory of the Midwest was held at various times by the French, Spanish, and English. The Northwest Territory – much of which had been opened by the early French trappers, traders, missionaries, and settlers – was acquired by the fledgling United States from England by the Treaty of Paris in 1783, and Ohio, Illinois, Indiana, Michigan, Wisconsin, and part of Minnesota were carved out of this area. The rest of Minnesota, along with the future states of North Dakota, South Dakota, Nebraska, Kansas, Iowa, and Missouri, were acquired from France in the Louisiana Purchase of 1803. Despite some fierce fighting over the issue, especially in Kansas, those Midwestern territories that entered the Union before the Civil War did so as free, not slave, states.

The Midwest's reputation as the center of the country's agricultural life is well founded: Pennsylvania may have been America's first breadbasket, but in the nineteenth century, that title moved steadily west along with a stream of settlers and homesteaders. Until then the Midwest had been an almost deserted wilderness, punctuated by a handful of frontier outposts. Some, like Ste. Genevieve, Missouri, and Vincennes, Indiana, still have some of the homes and churches built by the settlers who followed the first French Catholic missionaries and French, Spanish, and English explorers there. The Native Americans tried desperately to retain their homelands: the last major battle east of the Mississippi River that pitted Indians against settlers took place in 1811 in Tippecanoe County, Indiana. Seventy-nine years later the last great battle

Right: After General George Custer and his soldiers in 1874 confirmed the rumors that there was gold in the Black Hills of South Dakota prospectors and settlers streamed into the Dakotas. The Sioux fought back, most notably in 1876 at the Battle of the Little Bighorn, also known as "Custer's Last Stand." The Sioux won the battle, but the war and their land were probably already lost: towns like Deadwood were, as shown here, already burgeoning by 1876. The name "Deadwood" incidentally, referred to burnt-out trees a fire had left behind in a ravine that became the town's one through street. Deadwood soon became one of the legendary frontier towns: Wild Bill Hickok was sheriff there – until he was shot dead by Jack McCall during a poker game. Both Hickok and Calamity Jane (who claimed that she and Hickok were secretly married) are buried in Deadwood's Mount Moriah Cemetery.

Opposite: Deadwood today still has only one main street; the town both honors and exploits its frontier past via such enterprises as the Western Heritage Museum, the Adams Memorial Museum, the Broken Foot Gold Mine, and various saloons and gaming halls where betting on poker and blackjack is still legal.

between the Native Americans and the new Americans took place at Wounded Knee, South Dakota, on the westernmost borders of the Midwest.

In 1803, when President Jefferson sent Meriwether Lewis and William Clark on their historic trek in search of a viable land route to the Pacific coast, the explorers left from Saint Louis, already a center of the fur trade and soon to be known as the "Gateway to the West," a title once held by Pittsburgh. In 1808 the first newspaper published west of the Mississippi appeared in Saint Louis. In 1817 the first steamboat chuffed along the Mississippi into Saint Louis, and by 1820 there was regular stagecoach service from Louisville, Kentucky, to Vincennes, Indiana, and then on to Saint Louis.

By 1843 the country's center of gravity had shifted westward: almost one-quarter of the nation's 9,638,453 citizens now lived west of the Appalachians. Yet some areas of the Middlewest remained sparsely populated for years: there were only 500 settlers in North Dakota as late as 1870. By contrast, some 15,000 gold prospectors streamed into neighboring South Dakota in 1875-76, leading to the ill-fated military expedition that culminated in George Armstrong Custer's celebrated last stand near the Little Big Horn in the Black Hills in 1876.

After the Civil War railroad lines cut deep into the Midwest, linking such cities as Chicago and Abilene, Kansas, and making it possible to speed cattle from the plains around Abilene to the stockyards and slaughterhouses of Chicago. During the 1860s Chicago grew from a town of 30,000 to a city of some 112,000. The great fire of 1871 left 100,000 homeless, but a new Chicago, with many buildings designed by such architects as William Le Baron Jenney and Louis Sullivan (including the Home Insurance Building, Jenney's pioneering steel-skeleton skyscraper, built in 1883), quickly rose from the ashes, becoming the city that Carl Sandburg called "the Nation's Freight Handler."

Farming has always been so important in the Midwest that it is sometimes easy to overlook the equal importance of manufacturing to the region's economy. After about 1870 there was a steady shift of the nation's industrial base away from the Northeast and toward the Middlewest. By the early

twentieth century the heart of American heavy industry was located in a vast geographic belt that stretched across northern Ohio, Indiana, and Illinois, as well as reaching far up into Michigan and northwest into Wisconsin and south to St. Louis. Indeed, this is still the heartland of American industry, though since the 1960s its importance has somewhat declined as the overall American economy has shifted away from heavy industrial production, leaving cities like Detroit, once the automobile capital of the world, with many idle factories and giving rise to the lugubrious term "the Rust Belt."

The greatest symbol of Middlewestern industrial prowess is, of course, the automobile. It transformed the world, and it certainly transformed the

In 1779 Jean Baptiste Pointe du Sable built the first known permanent house in what is now Chicago, but the town was insignificant until canal and rail service linked it to the rest of the country in the 1850s. The Great Fire of 1871 destroyed 2,000 acres of Chicago but also made it possible for the town to be rebuilt from the ground up on modern principles of city planning. The next great period of growth in Chicago was the 1920s, when the produce market was moved out of the center of town and the area of Wacker Drive between Michigan and Wabash Avenues was rebuilt (opposite). The tall Mather Tower at 75 East Wacker Drive and, across the river, the white French Renaissance-style Wrigley Building, with its distinctive clock tower, were among the most notable structures of the era. Both still stand, now surrounded by sleeker, less distinctive new buildings (right).

Middlewest. Neat suburban developments made up of houses with one and sometimes two-car garages sprang up in former farmlands near cities and towns. the countryside sprouted drive-in restaurants, drive-in movies, and some of the country's first shopping malls, such as Northland, outside Detroit. Though most of the drive-in restaurants and movies that flourished in the 1950s and 1960s are gone today, they have simply been replaced by modern counterparts – fast food drive-through chains and multi-screen complexes in malls.

Earlier Midwestern hallmarks such as barn raisings and quilting parties have also largely vanished, but some small-town traditions still persist: ice cream socials at churches, Fourth of July parades, and 4-H Fairs. And, fortunately, the fact that Midwesterners take a good deal of pride in their local history has been a boon to the preservation movement. Cities such as Indianapolis, Indiana, have lovingly preserved old houses — Benjamin Harrison's house, for example, or the home of James Whitcomb Riley — that might never have survived had they been located in New York or Los Angeles.

Yet if the Midwest cherishes its past, it nevertheless looks enthusiastically to the future. In many cities, especially those not too heavily burdened with obsolescing industrial plants, there are growing signs of a return to that boom-town mentality that originally transformed a sprawling wilderness into an American "heartland" — in every sense of the term.

Union Station, which cost $65 million to build (opposite and left, above), was part of an ambitious 1920s urban renewal project known as "the plan of Chicago," which gave the city both a new train station and new post office and removed an awkward bend in the Chicago River. When Union Station was completed in 1924 an article in the *Chicagoan* boasted that there was no need for "No Spitting" signs in the terminal because would-be spitters would be deterred "by the sheer elegance of their environment." During the great days of train travel the six-square-block Union Station was, along with New York City's Grand Central and Pennsylvania stations, one of the country's busiest terminals. Just as passengers today flying between the east to the west coasts often have to change planes at Chicago's O'Hare Airport, train passengers changed at Union Station, many spending the night in Chicago and enjoying the fine hotels and shops in the nearby Loop district. Today, Amtrack trains pass through Union Station (left, below), whose handsome classical stone facade contrasts with the sheer glass and metal skyscrapers that now surround it.

104

Left and below: Chicago is defined by a river, a lake, and a park: the Chicago River, Lake Michigan, and Grant Park. The park stretches for some 200 acres along Lake Shore Drive between Michigan Avenue and Lake Michigan. In addition to its gardens and fountains, Grant Park contains virtually all of Chicago's important cultural institutions, most built between the 1890s and the 1930s: the Shedd Aquarium (left, under construction in 1928), the Adler Planetarium, the Field Museum of Natural History, the Public Library, the Art Institute, Orchestra Hall, the Fine Arts Building, and the Auditorium. Almost all these institutions were privately financed. The Shedd Aquarium was built with the $3 million gift of John G. Shedd, a president of Chicago's preeminent department store, Marshall Field and Company. The domed octagonal aquarium was finished in 1929 and opened to the public the next year. Today (below) its six galleries contain more than 500 species of fish, as well as a whole Caribbean coral reef.

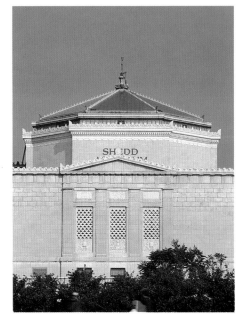

Left and above: Two views of the Chicago River. On the left is a 1930 view, looking west from the Michigan Avenue Bridge toward the then-new Wabash Avenue Bridge. The contemporary photo above shows part of the same area from another angle, a stretch of the river (and Wacker Drive) between the Michigan and Wabash Avenue bridges. The river is still an important commercial artery, for it is the first link in the vast chain of waterways that has, since 1933, connected the Great Lakes to the Gulf of Mexico.

Chicago has been nicknamed "The City that Works," and The City that Works takes its athletic teams seriously: the Bulls basketball and Black Hawks hockey teams now play at the Chicago Stadium (right). When sports events aren't taking place at the Stadium, things still can get lively: many political conventions, such as the 1932 Republican Presidential convention (above) that renominated Herbert Hoover, have been held here.

Chicago has two major league baseball teams: the White Sox, who play at Comisky Park and the Cubs, who play at Wrigley Field. The photo on the right, below, was taken in Wrigley Field during the 1929 World Series (A's:4; Cubs:1); the contemporary aerial view above it shows a night game in progress in Wrigley Field. One of the nation's oldest ball parks, Wrigley Field was built in Chicago's North End in 1914 on the former site of a seminary. It has been home to the Chicago Cubs since 1916. The field takes its name from the famous chewing gum family, which began to buy into the Cubs in 1916 and had a controlling interest in the team by 1921. An increasingly old-fashioned stadium, with a playing field of what has been called the most beautiful four acres of bluegrass in the world, with Boston ivy on the outfield wall, and with a manually operated scoreboard and no roof, Wrigley Field was the last major league stadium in the country to hold out against night games. The stadium was in fact set to get lights in 1941, but when the Japanese bombed Pearl Harbor, the Wrigleys donated the lights to the American war effort. There was no great local sentiment in favor of lights after the war, and as a result, the Cubs didn't begin to play home games under lights until August 8, 1988. Even then, some die-hard Cubs fans grumbled a bit, but that is nothing compared to what they would have to say if anyone ever proposed to turn Wrigley Field into yet another "superdome."

Twenty one million people visited the Columbian Exposition's "Great White City" in Chicago's Jackson Park in the summer of 1893 (below and opposite top left). Visitors gaped both at the daring belly dancing of "Little Egypt" and the ornate neo-classical architecture of the buildings that lined the lagoons and gardens designed by the great landscape architect Frederick Law Olmsted. The spectacle was so fabulous that one young man wrote home to his father, "sell the cook-stove if necessary and come. You must see this fair."

The Fine Art Palace (opposite, lower right) was one of the most impressive buildings in the great Columbian Exposition, and it is one of the few Exposition structures that still stands in Chicago (in Jackson Park). Its name and function have changed several times over the years: it was, for example, called the Field Museum when the photo opposite, upper right, was taken. Today (opposite, lower left) this huge 20-acre structure is Chicago's Museum of Science and Industry.

When Chicago's South Shore district was in its heyday in the 1930s and 1940s the South Shore Country Club (opposite, in 1936) epitomized elegance. The club itself dated back to 1906, and its neo-Spanish-style clubhouse was built in 1916. This was *the* spot for tea dancing and dinner dancing, for golf and sailing, a privileged enclave of upper-crust Chicago. But by the mid-twentieth century many South-Side residents were moving out of town to the suburbs, and the country club closed in 1974. The Chicago Park Department then bought the property, extended the lakeshore drive through the grounds, created a small artificial lagoon, and opened the once-exclusive clubhouse and grounds to the public. Today the complex of South Shore park grounds stretches down almost to the campus of the University of Chicago, which occupies some of the area once given over to the Columbian Exposition of 1893.

111

Chicago's motto is "Urbs in Horto:" the city in a garden. In addition to its great parks – Lincoln, Grant, Jackson, and Washington – Chicago has a number of smaller parks. Riverview Park (opposite, in 1931), with its daredevil loop-the-loop rides, was a popular North-Side amusement park in the 1920s and 1930s. Whole families came here to listen to school bands or to attend annual company picnics, such as the Crane Company's 75th anniversary picnic in 1925 (left). Today (above), Riverview is a quiet public park, with jogging paths along the river.

PHOTO BY J.W. TAYLOR
CHICAGO 1914

Midway Gardens (opposite, in 1914), with its bandshell, jazz music, cabaret performers, and dinner dancing under the stars, was once one of Chicago's favorite nightspots. It was designed in 1913-14 by a young man who would one day be called the greatest American architect of his generation, if not of all time: Frank Lloyd Wright. Even then Wright's distinctive style was evident in such details as the large rectangular flower vases, individual table-side lamps, long low-pitched roofs, and vertical light clusters. Midway Gardens finally closed in 1929 and was almost immediately torn down, to be replaced by a succession of garages and filling stations. Today the site is home to a modest apartment complex (left) – many of whose residents might well be astonished to learn that they are living on the site of a lost Frank Lloyd Wright creation, a place where Chicagoans once danced the night away to the music of such masters as Wingy Manone and Benny Goodman.

If Chicago's State Street ("that great street") has been immortalized in song, Michigan Avenue easily leads in the race for the most nicknames – the Miracle Mile, the Magnificent Mile, Boul Mich, and so on. The most elegant part of Michigan Avenue is the ten blocks south from the river to Oak Street, for here are many of the city's smartest shops, swankest hotels, and most prestigious offices. Some historians think that the first permanent structure in Chicago, Jean Baptiste Point Du Sable's cabin, may have been built on what is now Michigan Avenue, but in any case, the avenue has clearly been the heart of Chicago since well before the building of the Michigan Avenue Bridge in 1920. Small wonder that most parades in Chicago, such as the 1933 American Legion Parade shown on the right, march down Michigan Avenue, passing the Art Institute with its splendid bronze lions.

As long as there have been cars in Chicago, Michigan Avenue has been crowded, even as far back as 1918 (opposite top, right and left), when tin lizzies dropped visitors off for a day at the Art Institute.

Right: The Art Institute is still at the heart of Michigan Avenue, but a relative newcomer further down the avenue has put its mark on the Miracle Mile: Water Tower Place at 845 Michigan Avenue. This is the home of Chicago's grandest hotel, the Ritz-Carlton, and more than a hundred shops and restaurants. Water Tower Place was the prototype of such urban complexes as New York's Trump Tower, where waterfalls and gardens help browsers to forget the stress of urban life. This is especially appealing on Michigan Avenue, one of the windy city's coldest streets in winter.

The Art Institute was designed in the popular Beaux-Arts style in 1893 by the local firm of Shepley, Ryan, and Coolidge. The museum's collection can hold its own with that of virtually any other art museum in the world, its collection of nineteenth- and twentieth-century French painting being especially impressive. Generations of children (and their parents) have enjoyed the famous miniature rooms on view in the Thorne collection, and social and architectural historians are drawn here by the Art Institute's photo collection.

FERRY FIELD, ANN ARBOR, MICH.
PENNSYLVANIA vs MICHIGAN
– NOV. 16 - 1907 –

Above and left: Basketball, baseball, and football: the three quintessentially American games. And of these, football is *the* college game, and the Middle West's Big Ten is *the* college football conference. The University of Michigan has been a pillar of this conference since 1896 – before the term "Big Ten" was even coined. The photo above is of Ann Arbor's Ferry Field in 1907, taken during a game between Michigan and Pennsylvania (it was the only game Michigan lost that season). How far football has come since then is suggested by the photo on the left showing today's huge 106,000-seat Michigan Stadium.

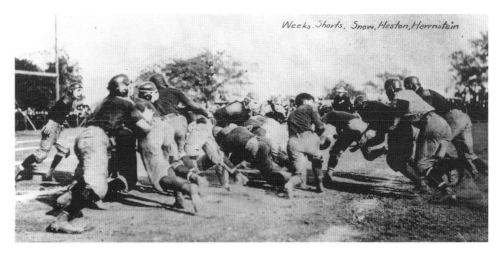

Weeks, Shorts, Snow, Heston, Herrnstein

Far right: The Michigan football varsity squad in 1897, the year after Michigan joined the ICFR, precursor of today's Big Ten. Michigan would win its first ICFR championship in 1898, and in 1901 it would acquire the now-legendary Fielding Yost as its head coach.

Above: Yost's "Point-a-Minute" teams of 1901-03 would enjoy an amazing 29-game winning streak, still the Big Ten record, and on New Year's Day, 1901, Yost's boys would defeat Stanford 49-0 in the first-ever Tournament of Roses Game held in Pasadena (above).

Right: Today almost everything about football has changed — its status and popularity, its rules, its settings, its uniforms (the modern kit shown here is worn by the outstanding 1990s Michigan quarterback Elvis Grbac) — but at mighty Michigan the spirited tradition of victory remains just the same as it was in the days of the Fielding Yost.

From the simple 1913 Ford factory in Dearborn, Michigan, shown above to a Nash factory during World War I (left) and a post-World War II Chevrolet factory turning out cars and trucks (center), the automotive assembly line has revolutionized American industry and production around the world. The first Model T Ford appeared in 1903. Just two years later, in 1905, there were 80,000 cars on the roads, Americans had stopped shouting "Get a Horse!" and the name of a city in Michigan, Detroit, was fast becoming a synonym for a revolution in human transportation.

Above and left: Today technological advances have created mixed blessings in the automotive (and, indeed, in every other) industry: thanks to robotics, fewer and fewer workers are needed. Robots may be ideally suited to do work which many people once found "mindless," but that is cold comfort for displaced workers who must now retrain for new jobs that may themselves soon enough become hostage to advancing technology.

Opposite: Springfield, Illinois, had not been founded when Illinois gained statehood in 1818, but by 1837 it was large enough to be chosen as the state capital. At once, work began on a domed State Capitol building, with a facade of locally-quarried limestone. This was where Abraham Lincoln gave his "House Divided" speech in 1858, and where his body lay in state after he was assassinated in 1865. In 1888 a new statehouse (far left, in the 1890s, and left, today) was built, and the old statehouse became a courthouse. The much-larger new building – its dome rises 405 feet above the ground – was the work of Chicago architect John C. Cochrane and is an ornate monument to another era's taste in civic buildings.

This page: In neighboring Indiana, Indianapolis was founded in 1820 to be the state capital; today, Indianapolis is one of the country's 50 largest cities and America's largest city without a navigable waterway. Like most American towns and cities, Indianapolis has its war monuments. Perhaps best known is the Soldiers' and Sailors' Monument: built in 1901, it is as much a focal point today (far right) as it was when the picture on the right was taken in the 1920s. At 258 feet, the monument once seemed imposingly tall, but neighboring modern highrises have done much to diminish that effect.

123

Above: The first Indianapolis 500 race took place at the Indianapolis Motor Speedway in 1911. The winning driver was Ray Harroun, and his Morman Wasp tore up the track at an average 74.59 mph.

Right: The mount of Indy star John Andretti typifies today's awesome racers, with their big turbo-supercharged V-8s, wings, fins, and aerodynamic side-pods. As of 1992, the Indy record stood at 185.984 mph.

Surrounded by Indiana farmland (top, left and right), the setting of the Indy 500 racetrack is only a little less bucolic now than it was 50 years ago. The track has seen many races that were almost too close to call. For example, in 1954 Bill Vukovich nosed out Jimmy Ryan and won the Indy 500 for the second year running (above). Vukovich's time of 130.840 mph was a new race track record.

The Indianapolis speedway is only 2½ miles long, so it takes a lot of laps before the 500-mile race held each Memorial Day Weekend is finished. The winning driver can earn as much as $5 million in prize money. About the closest finish ever was recorded in the 1992 race (above right), narrowly won by Al Unser, Jr.

The picture on the left, below, shows Saint Louis, Missouri, as it looked in the 1940s; it was then a big and important, but gently decaying, city. The two photos opposite show a reviving Saint Louis in the mid-1960s; the big new Busch Stadium is in place, and the huge 630-foot Gateway Arch, designed by Eero Saarinen, is just being completed. Framed by the arch is the stately Greek Revival Old Courthouse, where the first Dredd Scott trials were heard in 1847 and 1850. The contemporary view on the left shows Saint Louis's ultra-modern skyline today.

127

The contemporary picture above shows another view of the stainless steel Gateway Arch, this one looking from Saint Louis's Memorial Plaza toward the Old Courthouse and the Jefferson National Expansion Memorial park, where the gigantic arch stands overlooking the Mississippi.

128

South Dakota's first prosperity came from the furs that trappers and traders found there. Then gold was found in the Black Hills, and the gold rush brought a new flush of prosperity to the region. But the longest-lasting and most durable source of income has always been farming: 90 per cent of South Dakota is given over to farm land. The state's most flamboyant building, the Corn Palace on Main Street in Mitchell, South Dakota, gaudily celebrates that rural heritage (right, above, in 1955, and below, today). Mitchell's first Corn Palace was built in 1892 for South Dakota's Corn Belt Exposition. Later additions to the Corn Palace, the most recent in 1921, were in the spirit of the original building, a fantastic, Moorish-style structure with domes, turrets, and mosaics. In addition, each year the walls of the Corn Palace are decorated with elaborate murals made entirely of the local corn, hay, wheat, and oats that are such important crops in South Dakota. The Corn Palace Festival takes place each year during the last week in September to celebrate the new harvest.

It is hard to see how the old (opposite) and new (above) Statehouse buildings in Bismarck, North Dakota, could be more different in style and ornamentation. The original brick and stone structure, with its ecclectic Romanesque arches, classical portico, and stained glass windows, speaks clearly of the self-confidence of the late 1800s when it was built. The building might still be standing today, but it burned to the ground in 1930. The new capitol building, built during the depression years of 1933-35, is a sleek 19-storey skyscraper, faced in Indiana granite and commanding superb views across the Dakota plains.

If New York's Niagra Falls is the country's best-known natural wonder, South Dakota's Mount Rushmore may well be its most famous man-made wonder. The man in question was sculptor Gutzon Borglum (1867-1941), who was born in Idaho, studied in France, and sculpted the faces of Washington, Jefferson, Lincoln, and Theodore Roosevelt at Mount Rushmore. The upper picture on the left shows the state of the huge project in 1936, eleven years after it was begun. The picture opposite, right, shows work still in progress on Lincoln and Roosevelt in 1941. The color pictures lower left and opposite, left, are contemporary. Mount Rushmore was actually Borglum's second such undertaking: between 1916 and 1924 he worked intermittently on carving a monumental Confederate memorial out of Stone Mountain, Georgia. The project ended badly, and Borglum destroyed what he had done before beginning work on Mount Rushmore in 1925. Borglum intended to sculpt the presidents down to the waist, but he died before he could do so; his son, Lincoln, merely added some final touches to his father's work. The huge granite faces, which stand some 600 feet above the valley, are each about 60 feet high.

Verne's
Photo

132

This corduroy road (above) was laid in Deadwood, South Dakota, in 1876, the year both of Custer's Last Stand and of Wild Bill Hickok's death. Hickok, who had won fame as a sharpshooting U.S. marshal, was gunned down during a poker game at Deadwood's Saloon Number Ten. The upper center and upper right pictures show Deadwood in the 1940s: the process of exploiting the town's rowdy past as a tourist attraction has already begun.

Just as plainsman-turned-showman Buffalo Bill Cody found that he could turn an exaggerated version of his frontier past into a good source of income, many South Dakota towns like Deadwood today hotly pursue tourist dollars with gaudy – if not always authentic – recreations of frontier days and ways (opposite, bottom row).

THE SOUTHWEST

Probably no region of the United States — with the possible exception of the South — has laid claim to the nation's imagination as firmly as the Southwest. Americans who have never traveled west of the Hudson River feel that they know the Southwest, thanks to such movies as *Rio Grande*, *Fort Apache*, and *Stagecoach* — not to mention that quintessential American musical, *Oklahoma*. Songs and legends about tumbling tumbleweed and sagebrush, campfires, cowboys, and the Battle of the Alamo have made the Southwest familiar to generations of Americans who might otherwise have had trouble telling a Stetson from a Homburg.

It is hard to generalize about the landscape of the Southwest, which is generally considered to include Arizona, southern California, Nevada, New Mexico, Oklahoma, Texas, and Utah. This is a vast area (Texas alone is larger than all of New England combined with New York, Pennsylvania, and Ohio), and within it are high mountains, bleak deserts, prairies, and even cultivated lowlands.

Much of the Southwest is arid, with remarkably little annual rainfall; Death Valley, which runs between southern Nevada and southeastern California, regularly gets less rain than any other place in the United States, and in some years no rain at all. Yet aridity alone does not really define this varied region, cut by the Rio Grande and Colorado Rivers, which flow down from the Colorado's San Juan Mountains, at the Continental Divide. In New Mexico there are mountains rising to 13,000 feet, miles of barren flats like the White Sands Desert, and the spectacular Carlsbad Caverns, eerie limestone caves some 1000 feet beneath the earth. Arizona is, if possible, even more varied, with southern deserts, central plateaus and mountains, a petrified forest, the twisted spires of Monument Valley, and deep canyons formed by the Colorado River — including America's most famous natural wonder, the Grand Canyon.

Spanish explorers worked their way into the Southwest from Mexico in the sixteenth century, long before settlers arrived in New England or Virginia. Despite a string of forts and mission churches, along with a handful of settlements such as Santa Fe, founded in 1598, the Southwest remained sparsely settled until well into the nineteenth century. Without extensive irrigation, much of the land was neither arable nor hospitable. Furthermore, the early explorers were searching for the legendary Seven Cities of Cibola, hoping to discover the kind of wealth that they had found in Mexico and South America. When they failed to find signs of gold and silver, and Cibola proved to be only an agglomeration of Indian pueblo villages, the explorers abandoned the Southwest. For years to come the region was thought of as a bleak, uninhabitable land, suitable only for the Indians who lived in the pueblos of New Mexico and Arizona or roamed the Great Plains in search of buffalo.

The United States acquired Oklahoma in 1803 as part of the Louisiana Purchase and much of the rest of the Southwest at the end of the Mexican-American

Opposite: Palm Springs, California, as it looked 100 years ago – a desert at the foot of the San Jacinto Mountains.

Above: Today a showplace, Palm Springs has bloomed with irrigation, cultivation, and a massive influx of money. Its golf courses, swimming pools, parks, and gardens make it one of the nation's best-known winter resorts.

War in 1848. Texas – with California one of only two states to have been an independent republic – declared its independence from Mexico in 1836 and joined the Union in 1845. By then, although settlers had seen Texas's potential for cattle farming and had already founded Austin and Houston, much of the Southwest was still sparsely settled. Some trappers had moved into the area in search of beaver in the early nineteenth century after the supplies of beaver farther east were heavily depleted, but the fur trade proved short-lived. Settlement really began when cattlemen searching for new grazing lands began to move into the region. And there were other reasons for settlement as well: one of the earliest groups to move into the Southwest were the Mormons, who founded

Salt Lake City in 1847 in the hopes that its isolated site would allow them to live in peace, far from the suspicions of the non-believers.

Shortly after the end of the Mexican-American War in 1848 gold and silver were discovered in California and not long thereafter in several sites in the Southwest. Boom towns – many now ghost towns – such as Tombstone, Arizona, and Virginia City, Nevada, sprang up almost overnight. The mining boom was one of the reasons for the construction of the first transcontinental railway: on May 10, 1869 a golden spike linked the Union Pacific and Central Pacific lines near Ogden, Utah. Branching rail lines within the Southwest itself quickly multiplied when rich veins of copper were discovered in Arizona and New Mexico in the 1870s. Finally, in 1901, oil – known as "black gold" – was discovered in quantity in Oklahoma, just outside Tulsa, and in Texas, at Spindletop, near Houston.

The early Spanish explorers, so disappointed in their quest for the Seven Cities of Cibola, would have been astonished if they had known how much mineral wealth was actually located in the Southwest. But they might have been even more amazed if they could have seen how the desert would be made to bloom by irrigation. Two examples: one of the first things the Mormon settlers did was to irrigate the Salt Lake Valley for agriculture. And, in the 1860s, British engineer Darrell Duppa restored the extensive system of Indian irrigation canals in neighboring Arizona. Duppa predicted that a city would rise "phoenix-like" from the desert; it did: Phoenix is now Arizona's largest city.

On April 22, 1869, the Federal Government lifted its ban on settlement in the Indian Territory (which had been granted to the Native Americans "for eternity"). Homesteaders streamed across the Kansas border into Oklahoma: by nightfall on April 22 there were 15,000 settlers in the new town of Guthrie, Oklahoma. Not surprisingly, one of the first buildings built in Guthrie was a jail, for there were endless disputes about land rights. The up-beat lyrics of *Oklahoma* that urge the farmer and the cowman to be friends in fact allude to some extremely bitter – and often lethal – conflicts that pitted the sedentary farmers, with their fenced-in spreads, against the cattlemen who wanted to graze their herds freely across the Great Plains.

Much of the Southwest, especially Oklahoma, was devastated during the 1930s by the severe dust storms that turned acres of over-worked farmland into a "Dust Bowl." The damage was almost unimaginable: it is estimated that 50 million tons of Oklahoma top soil were blown away on one day alone. It has

136

Right: Las Vegas, Nevada, around 1910. Downtown was a lively mix of sundry stores that equipped miners and farmers, saloons, civic buildings, and land offices. Originally settled because of its mineral springs, Las Vegas prospered from nearby gold and silver fields. It became a major city after the construction of Hoover (then Boulder) Dam, which brought much-needed water for irrigation, in 1930. State legalization of gambling in 1931 was the largest single factor in the city's growth. Tourists poured in from southern California, and the resident population had reached almost half a million by the mid-1980s.

Right: Today "Las Vegas" conjures up images of glittering casinos, hotels, and nightclubs along "the Strip," the city's central avenue. An international airport brings visitors from around the world.

required sophisticated methods of land and water conservation and great public works such as the Hoover Dam to prevent repetitions of the Dust Bowl disaster.

The post-war years brought rapid development to the Southwest, making its cities among the fastest growing in the country: some entire new cities, such as Sun City, Arizona, were built for the thousands of retired Americans who settled there. Sophisticated scientific centers also began to spring up in the Southwest, including the Mayall Telescope in Arizona, the Array radio telescope complex in Socorro, New Mexico and the Sandia National Laboratory in Albuquerque, New Mexico. At the same time, major universities, such as the massive University of Texas at Austin, drew students from across the country.

Even the banking and oil recessions of the 1980s could not keep the Southwest from continued growth.

The "Sooners" and "Boomers", the miners and prospectors, not to mention the cowboys and gunslingers, have left the Southwest with a romantic aura that probably bears as little relation to the harsh realities of frontier life as the glitter of Las Vegas and Reno bears to every-day American life today. Yet it is still also true that the Southwest remains as variegated as its own scenery: a region big enough to have room for the oil fields of Oklahoma, the architecture and culture of the Spanish colonial past in Taos, the brash contemporary skyscrapers of Dallas – even corn that really does "grow as high as an elephant's eye."

138

Above: San Antonio's beautiful Paseo del Rio (Riverwalk) soon after its completion in 1941. The banks of the San Antonio River were landscaped and the river channeled through the city as a flood control project by the Depression-era Works Progress Administration. Architect Robert H. H. Hugman designed the winding stone paths along both sides of the stream, where cypress trees were transplanted from the Guadalupe River.

Opposite left: The Riverwalk, including 21 bridges in the downtown area, was designed to give this southern Texas town, founded in 1718, the feeling of an old Spanish city.

Opposite right: The early 1900s brought increasing growth and prosperity to San Antonio with the influx of Mexican nationals during and after the Mexican Revolution. The city's multicultural history is one of its major attractions.

An early-1900s postcard (above) shows Alamo Plaza in San Antonio, looking north toward the Alamo – originally the mission of San Antonio de Valero. This was one of five missions founded by Spanish Franciscans along the San Antonio River in the early 1700s. Like all the missions established from Mexico over a hundred-year period from 1680, its purpose was to convert the Indians to Catholicism and to extend Spanish influence in the New World.

At the left is the Alamo and its plaza during the 1920s, when San Antonio was almost 200 years old. It is the only major city in Texas that existed before the state won its independence from Mexico in 1836. During the 1920s the city grew rapidly, as thousands of Mexican nationals crossed the Rio Grande to escape the revolution. The city's prosperity owes much to the agricultural development of the Rio Grande Valley. The photo opposite, left, shows the carving on the weathered facade of the former mission church, now called the Shrine. It is typical of the Spanish missions of this era. Spanish craftsmen taught their skills to the local Payaya and Coahuiltecan, nomadic tribes who sought protection from the hard-riding Apache by working for the Franciscan missionaries.

Opposite right top: The Alamo compound includes the former church that fronts the plaza; the Long Barracks (formerly the Franciscan convent), where much of the fighting between Texans and Mexicans took place; and the surrounding grounds. The hopelessly uneven but courageous struggle between 188 defenders and 5,000 Mexican troops took place over a thirteen-day period in February/March 1836. The siege of American forces here was led by Mexican ruler and general Antonio López de Santa Anna, acting to put down the Texas rebellion against Mexican rule.

Opposite right bottom: In this 1920s photo it is clear that the upper part of the church was never finished. A stone church begun in 1744 on this site was destroyed by hurricane and fire, and the present church was begun in 1756. Local stone quarries produced the building material; the design was cruciform, with barrel vaults and buttresses. The mission was secularized in 1793 and received its present name (from the Spanish for cottonwood) in 1801, when a Spanish cavalry unit called El Alamo, for the Mexican town where they were stationed, was quartered here. The church was closed in 1812, and two years later, the former convent became San Antonio's first hospital.

142

Taos, New Mexico, was founded in Spain's northernmost American colony around 1615. Old elm and cottonwood trees shade the town plaza, which is ringed by adobe houses with their courtyards, and narrow, winding streets. Long an artists' colony, Taos is full of museums, studios, and galleries.

Above: As late as the early 1900s it seemed that Taos might be destined to remain an obscure little trading town well off the beaten track. But its natural setting, just west of the beautiful Sangre de Cristo Mountains in the upper Rio Grande Valley, and the proximity of ancient Taos Pueblo, drew many people to the remote region.

Left: Even in the 1940s old hitching posts were still in daily use in Taos for the workhorses and mules of local ranchers. Since then, however, new buildings have been carefully blended with Spanish-pueblo and frontier-style architecture to retain the flavor of the ancient town, which has become a popular tourist attraction without losing its identity.

In the 1903 photograph below Zuni water carriers display their traditional pottery. The pueblo Indians bore water up from springs at the base of their cliff dwellings, reached by ladders that could be drawn up for defense. The modern photo opposite, left, below is of a family from the Acoma Pueblo, called Sky City by the Spaniards, who scaled 300-foot cliffs to sack it. Acoma is believed to be the nation's oldest continuously inhabited town: it dates from A.D. 1200.

Above: In the early 1900s Taos Pueblo looked much as it had in 1540, when the *conquistadores* arrived. The sun-dried mud (adobe) of its walls was renewed over and over. The beehive ovens, called *hornos,* were adopted by Southwestern settlers as models for corner fireplaces that provided heat for the cold winter nights.

Right: Today many pueblo Indians maintain ancestral homes here, while living away from the pueblo. It remains the focal point of community life.

Above: Fifty years ago, members of the San Juan tribe performed the traditional deer dance, part of pueblo culture for centuries before the Hispanic and Anglo strands were woven into the tapestry of the Southwest.

Right: In recent years, Taos Pueblo has revitalized itself with an annual Powow celebrating the cultural heritage of the Southwestern pueblo. Gorgeously colored feather and bead work, and lavishly fringed buckskin, are among the skilled handicrafts worn by traditional dancers.

146

Above: Reno, Nevada, became well known as the city where out-of-state residents could obtain quick divorces under Nevada's liberal laws. In 1931 legalized gambling added to its attractions. This photo shows how gambling had affected the city's appearance by the 1940s.

Right: By the 1970s Reno had refurbished the sign that proclaims it "the biggest little city in the world" and had added scores of hotels and casinos to attract tourists from San Francisco and northern California. Reno had started as a railroad town in 1868 and had then become a banking and business center.

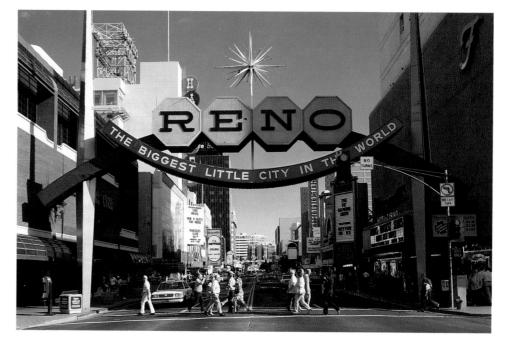

Above: Virginia Center, in Reno's hotel district, is the city's best-known venue. Tourism is Nevada's major industry, bringing in some $1.5 billion in revenue every year. Taxes on gambling account for almost half the state's total tax revenues.

Left: In the 1920s and 1930s Las Vegas, Nevada, grew rapidly because of, first, the construction of Boulder (now Hoover) Dam and, later, the legalization of gambling. Located in the southern corner of the state near the Colorado River, it was originally settled because of its mineral springs.

Bottom left: By the late 1950s, when this picture was taken, Las Vegas was host to the nation's best known and most expensive entertainers, and hotels like the Thunderbird were world famous. "The Strip" runs through what was once desert (and still is, beyond the city limits). By 1980 the resident population would increase to almost half a million.

Below: The improbable neon oasis of Las Vegas beckons like the gold and silver lodes that drew eager prospectors to this arid region more than 100 years ago,

147

Above: The nation's greatest natural wonder, the Grand Canyon of the Colorado River, was called by the native Havasupai "the house of stone and light." Travelers to the region were deterred by the canyon's depth (more than a mile at Point Imperial), its 10-mile width, and the cliffs that descend in gigantic steplike terraces to the river. These turn-of-the-century visitors were among the first to set foot in this area below Zoroaster Tower.

Opposite right: When Grand Canyon National Park opened in 1919 only 44,000 people visited the canyon, most of them by rail. The Desert View Watchtower, seen here, was designed by Mary Jane Colter. Hardier tourists descended the winding trails to the river on muleback.

Left and below: Ever since the Colorado River was dammed to regulate its flow, experienced boaters and kayakers have made pleasure trips – still strictly regulated – through the lower canyon. Even now, much of the river is unnavigable, with swift rapids and huge boulders in the riverbed. During floods, the crash of moving rocks is almost deafening.

Opposite below: John Wesley Powell was the first man to navigate the Colorado River through the Grand Canyon (1869). This picture is of one of his boats.

Above: Sheltered San Diego Bay has made this southern California city a useful port for half its history, which began in 1542 with the arrival of explorer Juan Rodriguez Cabrillo at Point Loma. This 1950s view toward the Civic Center at waterside shows the Spanish influence on local architecture. San Diego de Alcalá was the first California mission, founded in 1769.

Right: San Diego's skyline today shows the enormous growth of the city over the last 40 years: millions have moved into the area, and the naval and defense industries have expanded hugely.

Right: A U.S. Navy frigate enters San Diego Bay, one of the world's finest natural harbors. For many years, the navy's largest air station on the Pacific Coast was here on North Island. Established in 1917, it trained more than 31,000 pilots, bombardiers, gunners, and navigators during World War II.

Right below: A view of the harbor and North Island in 1929. In the background is Point Loma, with its national monument to founder Juan Cabrillo and the Old Spanish Lighthouse that is one of the city's landmarks. The temperate climate has made tourism an increasingly large component of San Diego's economy.

Above: The magnificent Hotel del Coronado, newly completed in 1913 and awaiting landscaping. Built on the sandy stretch called Coronado Beach, facing San Diego across the bay, the resort was the showplace of the fashionable San Diego hotel belt that grew to include La Jolla, Mission Bay Aquatic Park, and Oceanside.

Right: Thatched cabañas at Coronado Beach in about 1915. John Spreckels, a wealthy businessman, developed the Coronado area during the late 1800s.

Opposite left: The Hotel del Coronado has often served as a movie set for Hollywood, 75 miles north. In 1959 *Some Like It Hot*, with Marilyn Monroe and Tony Curtis, was filmed here by United Artists.

Opposite right: Impeccably refurbished and maintained, the Hotel del Coronado can hold its own against any resort on the Pacific Coast. Its grandeur is undimmed after 80 years as one of America's premier places in the sun.

153

Above: Across the San Pedro Channel from Los Angeles Harbor is Santa Catalina Island, a gathering place for Spanish pirates during the 1700s and for Hollywood stars, yachtsmen, and sport fishermen since the early 20th century. Its Avalon Bay was developed into a resort by William Wrigley, Jr., who bought much of the island in the 1920s.

Right: The deep-water harbor at Catalina crowded with steamships, ferries, and pleasure boats during the 1930s.

Opposite: The picturesque resort community of Avalon climbs the hill behind the bay, with its landmark circular marina. Douglas Fairbanks, Jr., and Joan Crawford spent their honeymoon at Catalina in 1928. Hollywood parties here could, and often did, go on for days.

Above: This gingerbread Main Street train depot delighted early visitors to Walt Disney's dream-come-true: the 180-acre Disneyland amusement park in Anaheim, California, 28 miles southeast of Los Angeles. Disney presided at the park's 1955 opening.

Above right: Exuberance was the keynote of Disneyland's 30th-anniversary celebration in the summer of 1985. Here Minnie Mouse heads up the big parade down Main Street.

Right: On July 17, 1955, as if by magic, the drawbridge to Fantasyland was lowered so that costumed Disney characters like Mickey and Donald could lead children into the courtyard and all the rides could come to life.

Opposite left: Disney characters, guests, and executives take part in the "Hands Across America" line in front of Sleeping Beauty Castle. Note the changes in Mickey's features and costume in this 1986 photo as compared to the 1955 photo of the park's opening.

Right: Anaheim's population soared in the decade after Disneyland came to town, bringing 90,000 new residents. Now (upper photo) the city's population stands at more than half a million. Once known primarily for its light industry and Valencia orange groves, Anaheim was still relatively urbanized when the lower photo was taken in 1956 (the Disneyland Hotel is under construction in a former orange grove in the foreground).

At the left is Los Angeles in 1885, looking east from the Courthouse. Settled by 11 families from Mexico in 1781, the city began to grow rapidly in 1870, with transcontinental rail travel. By 1890 the population had jumped from 5,000 to almost 100,000. By 1925 (bottom left) Los Angeles had sprawled out into most of the 30-mile region between the San Gabriel Mountains and the sea. The densely populated downtown was surrounded by streets filled with stucco and adobe bungalows, hotels and nightclubs, and the lavish homes of businessmen and movie stars.

Opposite right: A 1976 view of Los Angeles at dusk shows the skyscrapers that have sprung up to supersede 32-storey City Hall (distant white tower on right), once the tallest building in southern California. The high-rise buildings include the 62-story First Interstate Bank, the 52-story Bank of America tower, and the twin 44-story Century Plaza Towers.

Above: Today the Los Angeles skyline is dominated by the Library Tower, 1,017 feet high. The population has grown to well over 13 million, including Anaheim and Riverside. Over the years the city has annexed many other municipalities, including Van Nuys, Encino, Tarzana, Venice, Sawtelle, Hollywood, Bel Air, and San Pedro, now the port of Los Angeles.

160

Top left: The corner of Hollywood Boulevard and Vine Street — perhaps the most famous intersection in the world — is seen here in the mid-1920s. Hollywood was still surrounded by ranches, bean fields, and citrus groves.

Left: By 1946 Hollywood and Vine was bustling with postwar prosperity based on real estate, radio, and the movies.

Above: As Hollywood moved from village to metropolis, its great boulevard reflected the city's growth. During the 1950s its myriad bright lights seemed to be spelling out the message made famous on 1930s radio: "brought to you from Hollywood and Vine."

The Capitol Records Tower (above), whimsically shaped like a stack of records, rose at 1750 North Vine Street in 1955 to attest to the city's powerful role in the recording industry. Welton Becket was the architect. By this time, Hollywood Boulevard was a long, stately line of hotels, restaurants, apartment buildings, offices, and movie theaters. After a period of slow decline during the 1960s and 1970s, Hollywood Boulevard is today returning to its former grandeur. The Capitol Records Tower at Hollywood and Vine (left) stands as something of a symbol of this revival, reminding us that Los Angeles has never ceased to be the film-record-TV capital of the world.

162

Above: Horse-drawn vehicles were the main form of transport at Sixth Street and Broadway in 1890, but like most major U.S. cities, Los Angeles used electric trolley cars for urban transport well into the twentieth century.

Above right: By 1944 cars were taking over the same intersection and streets were being widened for heavier traffic. The war years made Los Angeles the nation's greatest industrial center after Detroit.

Over the past 40 years, Los Angeles has extended its huge network of freeways from the outskirts of the city to and through the city center. These high-speed, toll-free highways, with their many ramps and interchanges, are among the world's most heavily traveled roads.

Above: Hollywood's fanciful Chinese Theater, built for theater magnate Sid Grauman in 1927 and acquired by the Mann chain in 1972. Built at 6925 Hollywood Boulevard by developer C. R. Toberman, the flamboyant theater is a monument to the picture-palace days, complete with stone guard dogs, murals, columns, and Oriental vases and carpets.

Opposite left: In the tradition of Cecil B. DeMille's *King of Kings,* which opened the Chinese Theater in 1927, the Biblical epic *The Robe* had its swank premiere here in 1953. Cars agleam in the chrome of the era brought stars to view the production, filmed in highly touted CinemaScope.

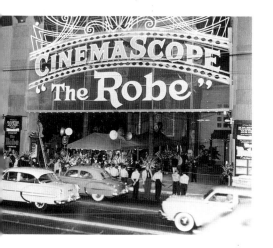

Top right: Sid Grauman's most brilliant publicity stunt was to have movie stars impress their handprints, footprints, and autographs in wet cement in the theater's forecourt. Here Marilyn Monroe and fellow pin-up Jane Russell do the honors in 1953.

Right: The palm-studded courtyard of Grauman's Chinese Theater, with its soaring pagoda roof, awed patrons of the late 1920s. Even for Hollywood, it was an extravaganza.

Far right: Besides the famous hand- and footprints, the Chinese Theater has immortalized in concrete John Wayne's fist, Harpo Marx's harp, Jimmy Durante's nose, and the hoofprints of Gene Autry's horse Champion and Roy Rogers' palomino Trigger.

Right: Hollywood and fashionable Westwood, between Beverly Hills and Santa Monica. Today Westwood Village has more first-run movie houses and studio premieres than any other part of Los Angeles. Beverly Hills is a separate municipality within the City of Angels.

Bottom right: Hollywood Boulevard and Western Avenue in the 1890s, when Hollywood was still a rural community.

Opposite left: The imposing Warner Bros. Studio in Burbank, California, purchased by the brothers after the success of their sound movie *The Jazz Singer* in 1927. The lot was originally built by silent-film producer First National in 1918. The Warners spent millions to redo the studio for talking pictures.

Opposite right top: The original studio established by Albert, Harry, Jack, and Sam Warner on Sunset Boulevard in 1918. The brothers were film distributors before they went into production.

Opposite right bottom: Youthful Bette Davis and Henry Fonda film Warner's *That Certain Woman* (1937). The studio prospered mightily throughout the decade, despite – or because of – the Great Depression, which sent millions to the movies for respite from everyday care. After Warner Bros. took over the former First National Studios in Burbank, the Sunset Boulevard lot was used to make the studio's popular cartoons featuring Bugs Bunny, Porky Pig, Daffy Duck and their friends.

166

Left: Ocean Boulevard in downtown Long Beach, California, just before the great 1933 earthquake that leveled much of the city and killed more than 50 people. Built along San Pedro Bay, 20 miles southeast of Los Angeles, Long Beach prospered as a seaport, tourist town, and oil producer. After rebuilding from the earthquake, it was a busy shipping center during World War II.

Bottom left: A hundred years after its founding, Long Beach is flourishing as part of the vast Los Angeles-Long Beach metropolitan area. It covers 50 square miles and has a population of almost 400,000. The city owes its growth to proximity to the port of Los Angeles, second only to San Francisco on the Pacific Coast.

Above: Forty years ago Pasadena was already the destination most coveted by college football teams. This attractive city 10 miles north of Los Angeles hosts California's best-known annual event on New Year's Day, when flower-strewn floats compete for prizes in the Tournament of Roses before the Rose Bowl football game. Western themes are always among the most popular.

Left: The Rose Parade gets bigger and more festive with the years, a source of civic pride to Pasadena and an exuberant celebration for visitors.

THE WEST

The fabled American "West," so celebrated in song and story, was always more an idea than a particular geographic region. The term really referred to the vast, amorphous western frontier and to the untamed lands that lay beyond it. But this frontier was never fixed, moving steadily westward from the Appalachians to the Pacific all through the nineteenth century. Thus there were times when the "West" was actually located in what we now consider the Middlewest, or the South — or even the East.

What we generally mean when we speak of the West today is the large and diverse region that includes both the Rocky Mountain states of Montana, Wyoming, Colorado, and Idaho and the Pacific Coast states of Washington, Oregon, and northern California. The two other "Western" states, Alaska and Hawaii, which joined the Union in 1959, are cut off from the rest of the region and have environments and histories largely separate from it. The environments and histories of the contiguous Western states, on the other hand, sometimes tend to blend somewhat into those of the neighboring Southwest: some of central California is physically akin to the desert regions of Arizona and Nevada, and several Western states have mountainous terrain similar to that found along the northern rim of the Southwest.

Just as plains and prairies define the Midwest's landscape, mountains and lakes dominate the West: Colorado alone has 53 mountain peaks rising at least 14,000 feet. The Rockies bisect Montana, Wyoming, and Colorado, while the barren Sierra Nevadas stretch almost the length of California before becoming the Cascade Range that runs from Northern California all the way to British Columbia. In Hawaii, a number of mountains are actually active volcanoes, notably Kilauea and Mauna Loa. Fittingly, the country's largest state — Alaska — also has its tallest mountain: the 20,320-foot Mount McKinley.

Before the nineteenth century the West was sparsely settled and imperfectly known. Only California, with its string of missions and garrisons founded after Juan Rodrigues Cabrillo and Bartolome Ferrelo explored the coast in 1542-3, had had any significant settlement before the nineteenth century. In the early years of that century, explorers such as Lewis and Clark (the first white men

known to have visited Idaho) and Zebulon Pike (after whom Pikes Peak is named) had considerably increased what was known about the West, yet even in 1820 Major Stephen H. Long could reconnoiter much of what is now Colorado, and report that the area was but a "Great American Desert . . . wholly unfit for habitation."

For the first half of the century such assessments of the West tended to discourage large-scale settlements, though some adventurous trailblazers such as Kit Carson did lead parties of exploration through the Rockies and Sierra Nevadas in the 1830s and 1840s. Fort Laramie, Wyoming's first permanent settlement, was founded in 1835, but its real importance was that it guarded the Oregon Trail west to the Pacific coast: some 400,000 pioneers passed by

Opposite: In 1888 Bodie, California, was a mining boom town. Most of its 168 buildings, including a Methodist Church and a Miner's Union Hall, were built before 1880.

Above: Today Bodie is a picturesque ghost town of empty streets and sagebrush, preserved as a State Historical Park. A few mining towns survived as supply centers for prospectors, even after their lodes were mined out.

Laramie in the 30 years from 1840-1870 as a steady stream of settlers headed west from the rowdy town of Independence, Missouri, along the Santa Fe and Oregon Trails. The settlers who made it to the Pacific Coast soon challenged the domination of the British Hudson's Bay Company in Oregon and Washington and began to farm and mine in California.

Three important enticements lured the pioneers west: the fur trade, cheap farmland and pasturage, and the chance of striking it rich by finding gold or silver. By and large, however, the East failed to take a serious interest in the West until gold was discovered, first in 1848 in California and then, 10 years later, in Colorado. Boom towns, with names like Boulder and Buckskin Joe that one could hardly imagine back East, sprang up wherever gold was found. Then, after the Gold Rush, came the Silver Rush, and it was only when the frenzy died down in the 1870s that the cattlemen began to move into the West. The 1880s were the epoch of the great cattle drives, when herds 50 miles wide were driven all the way from Texas to the pasturage of Montana. By then, with the completion of the Transcontinental Railroad in 1869 and the proliferation of rail spurs throughout the West, travel was no longer the ordeal that it had been for those who followed the Oregon and Santa Fe trails west.

Small settlements grew: By 1879 the mining town of Leadville, Colorado, was prosperous enough to have its own opera house. So, of course, did San Francisco, although for most of the nineteenth century the Bay City remained a

Opposite: San Francisco's historic North Waterfront has changed completely over the past 30 years, from a working waterfront to a tourist mecca and business center.

Below: A half-century ago the San Francisco waterfront teemed with the ferryboats and cargo ships that plied the 450-square-mile Bay. The city became the Gateway to the Pacific in 1869, when the transcontinental railroad was completed.

lawless, ramshackle town, repeatedly devastated by fires and earthquakes. Between the 1850s and 1876 Denver grew from an Indian encampment and frontier outpost to a city of 35,000. Denver's metamorphosis from Indian village into a thriving frontier settlement is a reminder of how the Native Americans were devastated by a series of military defeats and pushed on to ever smaller reservations: the victory over Custer in 1876 was indeed Pyrrhic.

In Alaska, Sitka was the only sizeable settlement before the United States purchased the territory from Russia in 1867; after gold was found near Juneau in 1880 and in the Klondike in 1896, miners streamed into Alaska. Today, of course, much of Alaska's wealth still comes from its mineral wealth, though now in the form of oil, transported to the rest of the nation through the Alaska pipeline. As for Hawaii, Protestant missionaries and those connected with the sugar trade were the most frequent foreign visitors there before the United States annexed the islands in 1898. Much of Hawaii's economy today rests on tourism: Honolulu's modern resort hotels draw visitors almost equally from Japan and the United States.

Because so much of the West was developed so recently – starting only in the Victorian Era – few areas of the country have better preserved neighborhoods, sometimes of turreted Queen Anne houses, sometimes of the gaily-painted wooden homes often called "Victorian Ladies." It is not unusual to find the oldest house in a Western town still in use. But in some towns, such as Virginia City, Montana, preservationists have united to preserve other relics of the past – livery stables, country stores, dance halls, and saloons – that flourished in the old boom-town days. And in California, Spanish missions are lovingly cared for in towns such as Santa Barbara, site of the Mission Santa Barbara (1786), whose beauty has earned it the nickname "Queen of the Missions."

Today, the scene of America's last frontier continues to be an area of rapid growth. Nothing, not even earthquakes, flash fires, and urban smog, has slowed California's pell mell expansion. And in recent years Oregon and Washington have begun to challenge California's reputation as the home of the zaniest new ideas, most innovative social programs, and most rapidly-changing skylines. The Seattle skyline, with its Space Needle, rivals San Francisco in its assemblage of stunning modern architecture, although nothing in the West as yet challenges Los Angeles for sheer urban sprawl, Yet perhaps the frontier has not wholly vanished after all, for in remote hamlets in Alaska modern-day pioneers still fight to hold their own against an encroaching wilderness.

Top left: The beauty of northern California's Yosemite Valley, seen here at 620-foot Bridalveil Fall, is viewed from a coach by turn-of-the-century travelers.

Left: Yosemite's major attractions include the groves of giant sequoias, up to 3,000 years old, that grow in the Sierra Nevada. Debonair tourists of 1904 pose at one of the gigantic trees.

Above: Contemporary tourists are equally intrigued by driving through the towering sequoias, which reach heights of 200 feet. The trees occur in three widely separated groves, forming shadowy stands so silent that one can hear a pine cone drop to the forest floor.

Above: The rustic Ahwahnee Hotel, built below the sheer granite face of Yosemite's Half Dome in 1927. Designed by Los Angeles architect Gilbert Stanley and constructed of stone and heavy timber, the hotel attracted wealthy travelers who wanted to rough it in style.

Left: The Ahwahnee Hotel today is essentially unchanged in the timeless serenity of its setting. During World War II the hotel served as a Naval hospital for convalescents. It was named for the native Ahwahneechee Indians, who spent summers in the Yosemite Valley harvesting acorns from the black oaks.

Above: San Francisco's Market Street, the main thoroughfare downtown, has undergone major renovation since 1971, from the Embarcadero, behind the waterfront, to Twin Peaks.

Left: Market Street as it looked in 1900, dominated by the domed Call Building, a municipal landmark since 1898. At this time, San Francisco had more than 300,000 residents. It had prospered by supplying prospectors in the 1849 Gold Rush, many of whom came back to settle with the fortunes they had made. When the Gold Rush began, the city had only 820 residents, 200 houses, two wharves, two hotels, and one newspaper.

Above and left: Market Street during the great earthquake of March 18, 1906. The first shock, at 5:13 A.M., damaged the water system, and toppling chimneys set fires that raged out of control. Whole blocks of buildings had to be dynamited to create a fire break, and the business district was largely destroyed. In the right foreground are personal belongings salvaged from the burning buildings.

Top left: The devastation caused by the earthquake is suggested by this photo of Market Street taken shortly before it occurred. Note the famed San Francisco cablecar in the foreground.

178

Top left: A view of modern San Francisco from Twin Peaks, located somewhat to the south on the peninsula occupied by the city. It was from a cottage on Twin Peaks that architect and city planner Daniel Burnham sketched the outline of a more orderly and beautiful San Francisco in 1905, the year before the earthquake. Some of his ideas were implemented when the city was rebuilt; others went by the board in the general haste to get the job done. Twin Peaks Boulevard, at Upper Market Street, offers a full 360° panorama of the city, whose boundaries are identical with those of San Francisco County.

Left: A view of San Francisco taken from another of its 42 hills in 1906. The extent of the damage caused by the earthquake is evident. Firemen and soldiers from the Presidio fought for three days to contain the fires that wiped out 497 blocks. Most of the buildings were two- and three-story wood-frame constructions.

Left: Pier 39, on Fisherman's Wharf, is the city's most-visited spot. Built in 1978 on the site of an abandoned cargo pier, its timbers were salvaged from the old working piers of the Northern Waterfront. The 45-acre complex includes dozens of luxurious shops and restaurants overlooking the Bay, with its sailboats and yachts. San Francisco faces the water on three sides. To the west is the Pacific Ocean; here, on the east, is San Francisco Bay, the world's largest natural harbor; and to the north is the Golden Gate Strait – the mile-wide channel that links the ocean to the bay.

Above: During the 1850s, wooden ships rotted at their moorings as crews abandoned them to follow the prospectors to the gold fields. A forest of masts crowded the harbor until the hulks were pulled ashore to serve as warehouses and even lodgings. Shopkeepers hung out signs that read, "Gone to the Diggings." It seemed that the whole city had left for Sutter's Mill on the American River, where James Marshall had discovered gold on January 24, 1848. It proved to be washings from California's Mother Lode, a vein of gold-bearing quartz that ran for 150 miles along the western foothills of the Sierra. When the prospectors came back with their wealth, San Francisco became the hub of the Golden West.

Opposite: A Chinese grocer at his stand in Chinatown around the turn of the century. Chinatown grew up around Portsmouth Square, the heart of San Francisco, during the 1850s.

Above and top right: At first known as "Little Canton," Chinatown grew rapidly, as some 15,000 Chinese sought their fortunes as miners, merchants, cooks, and restaurateurs. These street scenes from 1901 recall the period when the Chinese enclave was roughly two blocks long and six blocks wide.

Right: Now comprising 16 square blocks, Chinatown has the ambience of such major Chinese cities as Hong Kong, Taipei, and Shanghai. Here tourists shop on colorful Grant Avenue, the main street.

Far right: The jade-green, imperial Dragon Gate to Grant Avenue was a gift to San Francisco from Taiwan in 1971.

182

Above: San Francisco's cable cars were designed by local engineer Andrew S. Hallidie to travel the city's steep hills. They are powered by continuously moving cables under the streets. The first line, a successful experiment, ran between Kearny and Jones Streets.

Top right: Nob Hill was too steep to be readily accessible until the cable car came into service. Then it became the site of splendid mansions built by rich San Francisco businessmen, including Leland Stanford, James P. Flood, and Charles Crocker. Only the Flood mansion survived the earthquake to become, with additions by Willis Polk, the handsome Pacific Union Club.

Opposite: Downtown San Francisco moved steadily westward during the late 1800s, as the cable car made it possible to develop sites too steep for access by horse and wagon. By 1906 the area bounded by Divisadero on the west, the Bay on the north and east, and the region south of the original Mission San Francisco de Asís (Mission Dolores) was well established.

Right: An eagle's eye view of the Bay and Alcatraz Island from Car 12.

Above: Coit Tower, on Telegraph Hill, is a monument to San Francisco's volunteer firemen. The gleaming tower was built in 1933 at the behest of Lillie Hitchcock Coit, who had been the mascot of Knickerbocker Engine Co. No. 5 during her teens. Inside the 210-foot monument are murals by Depression-era artists. Their work on the theme of American labor was influenced by the frescoes of Diego Rivera. Originally, the Bay extended into the hollow between Telegraph and Russian Hills; thus the name North Beach for the lively Italian neighborhood that grew up in this vicinity.

Right: In 1898, when this picture was taken, Telegraph Hill was the inland terminus for the first West Coast telegraph, which originated at Point Lobos. It signaled the arrival of ships off the Golden Gate. On the present site of Coit Tower was a semaphore that could be seen by the merchants and shipping interests downtown. Telegraph Hill is now the site of Pioneer Park, with its entrance across from Coit Tower.

Top right: Alcatraz Island, "the Rock," was a formidable prison from 1912 to 1963. Surrounded by swift currents, and inaccessible except by boat, the waterless island of stone housed prisoners considered incorrigible by the Department of the Army and, after 1933, by the Federal Bureau of Prisons. The maximum-security cells measured only five by nine feet, and infractions of prison rules were punished by solitary confinement. Such notorious criminals as Al Capone, "Machine Gun" Kelly, and Bob Stroud, the "Birdman of Alcatraz," were confined here. There were no executions at Alcatraz, but there were nine escape attempts. The prison was closed in 1963, then seized by a group of American Indians, who claimed the unused island should revert to them by treaty. They occupied Alcatraz from 1969 until 1971, when a more radical faction took control until is was ousted by the Federal government.

Right: Today the island, operated by the National Park Service, is host to some 750,000 visitors a year. The bleak guard towers and empty cellblocks have a grim fascination for tourists.

185

Opposite: The recreation complex known as Cliff House Beach and Esplanade occupied part of San Francisco's western beach area, which stretches from Lincoln Park to Lake Merced, in the early 1900s. The property was first purchased by Prussian immigrant Adolf Sutro, who made a fortune from the Comstock Lode during the Gold Rush. In 1879 Sutro acquired the original Cliff House, built in 1863, and 1,000 acres of oceanfront on which he later built his own mansion and the famous Sutro Baths.

Top left: In their day, the Sutro Baths were the largest of their kind in the world. The huge bathhouse contained a series of six indoor pools containing both fresh and saltwater. Exotic objects of art and tropical plants filled the interior, and a number of outbuildings completed the complex. On the extreme right in this 1920s photo is Cliff House, in one of its many incarnations. Only ruins of the bathhouse now remain.

Bottom left: A much-remodeled Cliff House still clings to its site at 1090 Point Lobos Avenue, commanding views up and down the coast. The original Cliff House, purchased by Adolf Sutro in 1879, was demolished when a ship filled with dynamite struck the rocks below the building and exploded. Sutro rebuilt the house as a grand chateau raised above ground level, but the house burned down in 1907. Two years later the more modest basis for the present structure was built.

Above: Lombard Street, on Russian Hill, is famous as San Francisco's crookedest street. It has an 18.2 percent grade and eight turns in one block. Shrubs and flowers border the sharp S-curves.

Right: Only one side of Lombard Street has been developed in this 1945 photograph. On the other are houses still standing today, as seen in the color picture. San Francisco is well known for preserving and renovating its buildings.

Opposite: The challenge of Lombard Street proves irresistible to a group of motorcyclists in the late 1920s.

Top left: The original San Francisco Ferry Building. Designed by A. Page Brown in 1896, it served Oakland, Alameda, and Berkeley.

Above: By 1924 the Ferry Building, which survived the earthquake, had been greatly enlarged. Before the Bay bridges were built, it was the second busiest passenger terminal in the world.

Left: Located at Market Street and the Embarcadero, the Ferry Building was the hub of San Francisco's transportation pattern. Trans-bay commuters arrived by water directly to the city's heart and dispersed to their destinations easily by ground transportation. This photograph from 1941 shows that only the four-faced clock on the tower remains from the original building.

Right: I. M. Pei designed an adaptive reuse project for the Ferry Building site in the 1980s. Ferries still operate between Tiburon and Sausalito.

Below: An aerial view of the site during the 1930s, when the Bay bridges were under construction.

Opposite: The 4200-foot Golden Gate
Bridge was nearing completion in 1936.
Irving Morrow was the consulting
architect for this landmark suspension
bridge, the world's longest until 1959.
Two years after the bridge opened, San
Francisco held the Golden Gate
International Exposition of 1939. Called
"the World's Fair of the West," it was
attended by more than 17 million.

Above: Joseph Strauss, Chief Engineer, was
responsible for the great achievement of
placing tower foundations in the turbulent
currents of the Golden Gate. This 1934
photograph shows the Marin Headlands
tower, as seen from the San Francisco side.
Below the tower, a steamer bound for the
Orient glides through the Golden Gate to
the Pacific.

Right: By night, the great red bridge,
with its elegant Moderne detailing, is an
unforgettable sight.

Left: A rodeo rider of the early 1900s displays his skill at staying astride a bucking bronco, using only one hand to grasp the pommel of his saddle.

Far left: Cowboys confer at a waterhole after a long day riding herd on 15,000 cattle during a trail drive from New Mexico to the railhead in Sterling, Kansas, in 1898. The demand for beef in Eastern markets was such that cattle were called "gold on the hoof."

Bottom left: Cattlemen rope a steer for branding in the round-up town of Little Cove, Colorado, during the late 1800s. By this time, farmers were fencing off more and more land with barbed wire to keep marauding livestock out of their wheat and corn. Cowboys were losing ground to the "sodbusters," and there was bitter conflict between the two groups.

194

Top left: By 1990 rodeo rules hadn't changed: bronco riders still had to keep one hand aloft while clinging to their mounts. This Houston rodeo was attended by dignitaries in town for a summit meeting, including, center, President George Bush and his wife Barbara, flanked by Prime Ministers Brian Mulroney of Canada and Margaret Thatcher of Great Britain.

Above: Cowboys still work ranches in California, Oregon, and other cattle-raising states, doing many of the same tasks they did a hundred years ago, like calf-roping at round-ups. Today their most important tool, the rope, is made of nylon instead of horsehair, grass, or hennequin.

Left: A helicopter takes part in a wild horse "gather" in Lessen County, California. They are also used for locating stray cattle on huge ranches.

Above: Chestnut Street in Leadville, Colorado, shortly after the discovery of rich silver-lead mines brought thousands of fortune seekers to the area in 1878.

Opposite top and bottom: Leadville's Harrison Avenue appears to have changed only superficially in the past 100 years. Leadville once prospered from mining of gold, copper, iron, and molybdenum. It is sometimes called Cloud City because of its 10,200-foot height above sea level in the Colorado Rockies.

198

Far left top: The cornerstone for the granite State Capitol building at Denver, Colorado, is laid in 1890, nine years after the Mile High City was named the permanent capital. Founded during the Pikes Peak Gold Rush of 1858, Denver grew rapidly as a mining and transportation center.

Top left: Eleven years in the building (to 1901), the State Capitol has a gold-leafed dome that rises majestically over the heart of the city. It recalls Denver's history as a mining town. Today it is manufacturing that is the city's most important industry. Legend has it that Denver got its start when gold was "dug with a hatchet in Cherry Creek and washed out into a frying pan."

Bottom left: In 1958 Denver memorialized its first state capitol building – a log cabin built in 1859 – on the grounds of the imposing Capitol that has been in use for more than 90 years.

Top left: Denver's skyline appears beyond the trees in this view taken from City Park in the early 1900s. In the distance is Mount Evans in the Colorado Rockies, which rise 10 miles east of the city. At the far left is the dome of the State Capitol. At this time, Denver was already well known for its municipal park system, which was considered the nation's finest. The city's broad, well-planned streets and gardens, and its excellent climate, made it a popular tourist center and health resort.

Left: A contemporary view from City Park shows how Denver has grown during its second century as a city. Downtown now has a dozen buildings more than 30 storyes high, and over half the state's population is concentrated there. The city operates a chain of mountain parks covering more than 32 square miles in the Rockies. Tourism is more important than ever.

Above: A panoramic view of Denver in the 1890s, including the Capitol (center). On the right is 16th Street, a major thoroughfare.

Top right: Denver's early settlers wouldn't know what to make of 16th Street today: a manicured mall for pedestrian shoppers and the occasional mounted policeman.

Opposite: Cars and streetcars have taken over 16th Street in this 1930s photograph, which shows the Daniels & Fisher Tower, with clock, in the middle distance on the right. The tower has been a landmark since 1911.

Right: The Daniels & Fisher Tower shortly after its dedication, before horse-and-wagon transport downtown became part of Denver's history.

202

Above: A view from the esplanade in front of Denver's Union Station through the Welcome Arch to 17th Street. Erected in 1906, the arch weighed 70 tons and was illuminated by 1,600 light bulbs. The City of Denver paid $22,000 for the arch, which originally read "Welcome" on both sides.

Top right: In 1908 the 17th-Street side of the arch was changed to read "Mizpah" – a Hebrew blessing of farewell from the Book of Genesis (31:49). The center section of the "railroad Gothic-stlye" station seen here was used to create the present Union Station in 1912.

Right: Union Station itself, as it was between 1894 and 1912, when its size was reduced by the Denver Union Terminal Railway Company.

Union Station is still a handsome point of
entry into Denver for rail travelers.
Unfortunately, the Welcome Arch was
dismantled in 1931 as an impediment to
traffic.

Left: Aspen, Colorado, as seen from Aspen Mountain about 1900. This mining town in the Colorado Rockies scrambled into being in 1879, when prospectors found silver on the slopes of the mountain. Ten years later, Aspen had 15,000 inhabitants. The silver mines proved incredibly rich: one of them produced a single nugget of nearly pure silver that weighed just shy of a ton.

Opposite bottom: By 1910 the former boom town, seen here with Aspen Mountain in the background, had declined, as silver became less important to the currency. Mines closed, banks failed, and townspeople left this mountain-rimmed valley by the thousands. Only 700 would remain by the late 1930s.

Below: Aspen came back to life as a year-round resort during the 1940s, after a Swiss expert advised that the site was ideal for skiing. Now it is the nation's pre-eminent ski town, catering to wealthy tourists with such amenities as llama carriage rides. Luxury shops and condominiums attract celebrities, who come to enjoy the summer music festival and winter sports.

Bottom left: Aspen's lively nightlife includes elegant hotels, nightclubs, lounges, almost a hundred restaurants, and performances in the renovated old-time Wheeler Opera House.

Below: Turn-of-the-century Aspen under deep snow, with the Paragon Building, at left, facing Hyman Avenue. Victorian landmarks like this have been preserved and converted to new uses.

205

Right: A contemporary skier dressed for the slopes at Cooper Mountain, Colorado. Lightweight, colorful ski clothes have become the norm, and equipment is available in a bewildering variety of shapes and sizes.

Below: Eager novices of the 1920s turn out in everything from knickers to cloche hats, clutching cane and bamboo ski poles.

Below right: Western skiing at resorts like Aspen started to become popular during the 1940s. The costumes worn by U.S. skiers then were still largely based on styles evolved in Europe a decade earlier (shown here), as, indeed, was most of the equipment.

Above: Central City, Colorado, flourished as a mining town during the 1880s. When the gold ran out, it became a ghost town.

Left: More fortunate than most boom-to-bust towns, Central City made a comeback as a summer resort, with an annual opera festival, and as a winter playground. It is now one of Colorado's major tourist centers.

Right: The Mormon Temple in Salt Lake City, Utah, with the Brigham Young Monument in the foreground, is unchanged since its completion in 1893. Its tallest spire rises to a height of 210 feet over Temple Square. The gray-granite temple was designed by architect Truman O. Angell, a brother-in-law of Brigham Young, who led the Mormons to Utah. Ground was broken in 1853, and it took 40 years to complete construction.

Below: A view of 10-acre Temple Square in the 1930s shows the Assembly Hall at the left, with the Latter Day Saints Museum to its right. In the center is the Tabernacle. On the Temple, to its right, the highest spire bears a gold-leafed statue of the angel Moroni, who gave to prophet Joseph Smith the golden tablets on which the *Book of Mormon* was written. The Tabernacle became famous for the 325-voice Mormon Tabernacle Choir, which has sung here since 1867.

Above: The railway bed of the unfinished Union Pacific Railroad, thrusting west from Omaha in 1866.

Top right: The historic A. J. Russell photograph of the Union Pacific and Central Pacific meeting at Promontory, Utah, on May 10, 1869. A golden spike hammered in by a silver maul symbolized completion of the nation's first transcontinental railroad.

Right: Promontory had its day of glory, then faded away when the transcontinental junction was moved to Ogden, Utah. However, there is a colorful re-enactment of the event every year at the Golden Spike National Historic Site, now an expanse of sand and sagebrush.

Opposite: Five-hundred-foot Smith Tower was Seattle's tallest building when this picture was taken in 1914. It overlooks the seven hills on which Seattle grew up along Elliott Bay after 1852. The small port prospered as a result of the gold rush to the Yukon and Alaska that began in 1897. In the photo's background is Mt. Rainier, part of the Cascade Range, the city's best-known landmark.

Top left: Smith Tower and adjacent downtown buildings as seen from the city's harbor on Puget Sound during the 1950s. The city's rate of growth accelerated during World War II, when it served as an important shipbuilding and aircraft construction center. Left of the wharves is one of the large ferries that play a vital part in Seattle's transportation system.

Bottom left: Seattle's skyline has changed dramatically as it grew into the business center of the Northwest and the fourth largest containerized seaport in the country. The city's tallest building now is the 76-story Columbia Seafirst Center.

212

Opposite: The future site of Grand Coulee Dam, on the Columbia River in eastern Washington, is seen in this 1936 photograph. The great gorge called the Grand Coulee was the Columbia's riverbed during the Ice Age. It provided a natural reservoir and channel by which water could be diverted from the Columbia River into the arid lands to be irrigated by the Columbia Basin project.

Above: Grand Coulee Dam, completed in 1943, is the world's largest concrete dam, utilizing 4,400,000 cubic yards of concrete in its construction. Its spillways carry water from the West's greatest river to a vast area cut off from adequate rainfall by the Cascade range.

Above: In the early 1900s Juneau, Alaska, a deep-water port on the Panhandle at the foot of Mt. Juneau, had fishing and mining as its main activities. The town was founded in 1880, when prospector Joe Juneau found gold in the area – a strike so rich that $150,000,000-worth of gold would be mined here by 1944, when operations ceased. Meanwhile, Juneau had become the state's capital and one of its most important ports.

Right: Luxury liners dock at Juneau's new waterfront on their way through Alaska's Inside Passage. The city has become a major tourist center over the past 30 years because of its scenic location, the proximity of the Mendenhall Glacier, and the easy access it provides to fjords along the Gastineau Channel.

Left: Old buildings in downtown Juneau have been renovated into gift shops and restaurants for seagoing travelers. Like other Alaskan cities, including Anchorage, the state's largest, Juneau relies heavily on air and water transportation. The difficulty of building roads here due to severe weather, rugged terrain, water barriers, and permafrost means that most communities are not connected by highways.

Above: Juneau's Seward Street was paved with planking in 1914 on account of the mud. Eating places and stores catered to the miners at what was then the biggest gold mine in America.

216

Opposite top: The surprise attack on the U.S. Pacific Fleet at Pearl Harbor, Hawaii, on December 7, 1941, as recorded by a Japanese bomber pilot with a 16mm movie camera.

Opposite bottom: The battleship USS *Arizona* burns in Pearl Harbor after the bombing. The seven American battleships in the harbor were the chief targets among the 94 naval vessels anchored there. Japanese carriers commanded by Vice-Admiral Chuichi Nagumo had steamed to within 200 miles of Oahu under cover of darkness to launch the strike force of 360 planes.

Near left: For more than 18 years, the partly submerged USS *Arizona*, in which more than a thousand men were entombed, was visible on the floor of the harbor. A memorial to those who had died was finally built over the battleship in 1962.

Top right: Pearl Harbor is still the center of U.S. naval power in the Pacific. Formed by two mouths of the narrow Pearl Stream, it occupies about 10 square miles. A mile-wide entrance connects the landlocked harbor with the Pacific.

Bottom right: The USS *Arizona* memorial is a place of pilgrimage for veterans of World War II and other visitors to Oahu.

Left: Honolulu's Waikiki Beach, on Oahu, has kept its beauty despite the build-up of the city since World War II. Hotels stretch out in a long line toward Diamond Head, east of Honolulu's city center. Almost 80 percent of Hawaii's population is concentrated here at the state capital, and visitors come in greater numbers than ever to enjoy the legendary beach, with its surf riders and sailboats.

Above: Tourists at Waikiki during the 1930s look toward Diamond Head, an extinct volcano 760 feet high that is Hawaii's best-known landmark. Cruise ships brought wealthy, well-dressed travelers to the islands from the late nineteenth century on.

Opposite: Some 40,000 tourists visited Waikiki each year during the 1930s, even though there were then only a few luxury hotels on the beach.

220

Above: The famous Royal Hawaiian Hotel was built on Waikiki in 1927. It was a byword for elegance and the center of Hawaii's tourist trade for a generation. Its stately pink towers presided over the beach in regal splendor.

Opposite: Today the Royal Hawaiian is dwarfed by the modern high-rise hotels on either side, built to keep pace with Hawaii's $4 billion tourist industry, which has displaced agriculture as the cornerstone of the state's economy.

223

PHOTO CREDITS

All photographs courtesy of THE BETTMANN ARCHIVE and UPI/BETTMANN NEWSPHOTOS except the following:
ALPHA: Carlos Elmer: 139(left).
D. G. ARNOLD: 207(bottom).*
ASPEN HISTORICAL SOCIETY: 204(both), 205(bottom right).*
SUSAN BERNSTEIN: 36(bottom), 41(bottom), 45(bottom left, bottom right), 55, 79(bottom right).
TOM CARROLL PHOTOGRAPHY: 179(bottom left).*
CHICAGO HISTORICAL SOCIETY: 103(top), 104(left), 106(top), 109(top right), 110, 112, 113(bottom), 114, 116.
COLORADO HISTORICAL SOCIETY: 197(bottom), 198(top left, bottom), 200(top left, bottom right), 202(all three).
DENVER PUBLIC LIBRARY, WESTERN HISTORY DEPARTMENT: 196, 207(top).
D.J.A./S. D. TOURISM: 133(bottom right).*
JOHN F. DUNN: 73, 85(top).*
ESBIN/ANDERSON: 48(right), 50(bottom left, bottom right); Ruth I. Anderson: 43(bottom left); Bruce M. Espin: 47.*
DALE FISHER: 118(bottom).*
FLORIDA IMAGE FILE: Scott Key: 96(right).*
FORD PHOTO: 1(top).
HILLSTROM STOCK PHOTO: Gail Greig: 59(bottom); Ray Hillstrom, Jr: 6, 101, 103(bottom), 104(right), 106(bottom), 109(bottom left), 115(both), 197(top); Fred Natkevi: 117(bottom center); Raymond Prucha: 131(left); James P. Rowan: 91(right), 151(top); James Simon: 184(top).
HENRY E. HUNTINGTON LIBRARY AND ART GALLERY, SAN MARINO, CA: 170.
IMS PHOTO: Bill Watson: 125(bottom right); Dave Willoughby: 125(top right).
KANSAS STATE HISTORICAL SOCIETY, TOPEKA, KS: 194(top left).

COLLECTION OF JOHN KELLY: 140(top right).
LISA LAW: 145(right).
LIBRARY OF CONGRESS: 4, 144(bottom right).
JEAN MARTIN: 144(bottom left), 145(bottom left), 149(all three).
JAMES M. MEJUTO: 49(bottom), 52(bottom), 58(right).*
SUSANNA MILLMAN: 142.*
MUSEUM OF THE CITY OF NEW YORK, PHOTO LIBRARY DEPARTMENT: 45(top left).
MUSEUM OF MODERN ART/FILM STILLS ARCHIVES: 167(top right).
NAISMITH MEMORIAL BASKETBALL HALL OF FAME, THE EDWARD J. AND GENA G. HICKOX LIBRARY: 32, 33(top).
NATIONAL ARCHIVES: 38(top).
NATIONAL FILM ARCHIVE, LONDON: 165(left center).
NATIONAL PARK SERVICE, SHERMAN COLLECTION: 63(bottom right).
NEW ENGLAND STOCK: Bachmann: 89(bottom right); Dan Beigel: 75(bottom); Thomas P. Benincas, Jr: 20, 37(top left, top right); Roger Bickel: 16(bottom), 86(bottom), 129(bottom), 141(top right), 178(top), 185(bottom), 208(top), 213, 221; David A. Brown: 66(top right, bottom right); Kip Brundage: 39(top); Hannah Clements: 24(bottom), 25(bottom); Alan Detrick: 41(top), 57(right), 65(bottom left); Catherine L. Doran: 205(top); Alison Forbes: 211(bottom); Robert Hahn: 29(bottom); Martin E. Harwood: 17(bottom); Jean Higgins: 217(top); Michael Howell: 193(right); Howard Karger: 34(bottom right); Grant Klotz: 214(bottom), 215(bottom); Tony LaGruth: 2(top). 61(right), 63(bottom left); Clark S. Linehan: 29(top left, top right), 33(bottom); Michael Lottinville: 75(top); Bill Melton: 61(left); Thomas H. Mitchell: 19(bottom); Barbara Moore: 81(bottom left), 91(bottom); David E. Rowley: 173,

175(bottom), 182(bottom right), 195(bottom); Jim Schwabel: 30, 77(left), 85(bottom), 92(both), 94, 105(right); Frank Siteman: 27.
THE NEW-YORK HISTORICAL SOCIETY: 40.
COURTESY OF PENNZOIL: 124(bottom).
PHOTO NETWORK: Steve August: 187(bottom); Bachmann: 165(bottom right); Nancy Hoyt Belcher: 89(bottom left), 182(top right), 199(bottom); Barbara Benner: 217(bottom); Kevin Caldwell: 153(top), 161(bottom left); Tom Campbell: 171; Grace Davies: 63(top); Lonnie Duka: 168(bottom); Chad Ehlers: 150(bottom), 135, 154(top); T. J. Florian: 164, 181(bottom right); Dennis Giampaolo: 166(top); Dianne Leggett: 174(right); Earshal Long: 167(left center), 176(right); Michael Philip Manheim: 205(bottom left); John McMahon: 169(bottom); Margo Taussig Pinkerton: 79(top); Todd Powell: 108(bottomleft); Mark Sherman: 121(both); Marcia Wertenberger: 153(bottom); David Wheelock: 195(top right).
RAINBOW: Larry Brownstein: 10, 163; T. J. Florian: 43(bottom right), 69, 147(bottom right), 159; Dan McCoy: 8; Chris Rogers: 198(top right), 200(top right), 203.*
ROOT RESOURCES: Betty Kubis: 129(left); Dennis MacDonald: 122(right).*
TIM SCHOON: 98, 133(bottom left, bottom center).*
CAROL SIMOWITZ: 188(top), 191(top).*
SOUTHERN STOCK: John Anderson: 97(top); James Blank: 97(bottom right), 127(top left), 137; Pat Canova: 90(both); J. Christopher: 22; Mark E. Gibson: 35(bottom), 123(right), 127(right); Reed Kaestner: 218(left); Ralph Krubner: 146(right); Steve Lucas: 96(top); Jim Pickerell: 83(bottom); Todd Powell: 206(top); Les Riess: 87(bottom); Jon Riley: 39(bottom); Pete Saloutos: 130(bottom); Jim Schwabel: 80(top).
JOHN TELFORD: 209(bottom).*
TIGERHILL PHOTOGRAPHY: 111,

113(top).*
UNIVERSITY OF MICHIGAN, BENTLEY HISTORIC LIBRARY: 118-119(top), 119(top right, bottom left).
UNIVERSITY OF WYOMING, AMERICAN HERITAGE CENTER: 194(bottom).
JOHN WANAMAKER/BISON ARCHIVES: 167(bottom right).
WILLIAM WRENN: 12, 15, 53(right), 70.*
GEORGE ZENO COLLECTION: 165(top right).

*Courtesy, HILLSTROM STOCK PHOTO

ACKNOWLEDGEMENTS

The publishers would like to thank those who helped in the making of this book: Alan Gooch of Design 23, who designed it, Rita Longabucco and Elizabeth Montgomery, who did the photo research, and Elizabeth McCarthy, who prepared the index. We should also like to give a special thanks to David Greenstein and his staff at UPI/Bettmann for their help and the use of their wonderful collection of photographs.